GOING IT ALONE

GOING IT

ALONE

by
George Willig
and
Drew Bergman

A Dolphin Book
Doubleday
Garden City,
New York
1979

Art Director: J.C. Suarès
Designer: Amy deNeergaard
Production: Amy deNeergaard
        Ken Kleppert

ISBN: 0-385-14726-0
Library of Congress Catalog Card Number 78-24839

"Security and luxury shield one off from life. You never see the sky until you've looked upward to the stars for safety. You never feel the air until you've been shaken by its storms. You can never understand the ocean until you've been alone in its solitude. To appreciate fully, you must have intercourse with the elements themselves, know their whims, their beauties, their dangers. Then, every tissue of your being sees and feels, then body, mind, and spirit are as one."

—Charles A. Lindbergh,
The Spirit of St. Louis

At 4:30 A.M., when the alarm rings, I am already awake, and have been for hours. Well, I think. Here it is. All night long I have been tossing around, churning with what lay ahead. Although the night is not warm, I am drenched in sweat. There are so many questions, and the same ones circle round and round, carrying me with them, making sleep impossible.

What will happen up there? What will it be like? Will I make it? What will the police do? Will I be strong enough? Have I forgotten anything? Will my devices fail? Will I fall?

As it happens, falling is last (and least) of my worries, as it would be anticipating any other climb. What really does frighten me is the possibility—which I cannot control—that I'll be apprehended before I am even up on the building, and that a year of painstaking work and dreaming will come to a stunted, ignominious end. Far more nightmarish than anything else I imagine occurring on the sheer wall of the tower is the thought that I might be on the ground poised to go, feel a firm hand close on my arm, and hear "All right, buddy. Come along with me." And that will be the end of it.

The next night, where will I be? It is a toss-up, I think, between Bellevue Hospital, where I imagine a battery of bewildered psychiatrists interviewing me, and a jail cell. Although I do not think I will be treated like a hardened criminal, I cannot be sure. It is certainly a possibility I must acknowledge. Neither prospect appeals much.

It was all a mystery, and would be until morning, and so, although the physical demands ahead of me made it imperative I get some rest, I lay staring at the ceiling, buffeted like a pinball among the many unknowns, falling into fitful sleep for no more than an hour. The night was a long tunnel leading to the northeast corner of the south tower of the second tallest building in the world. I had begun my march through it, and, more than a little, I felt like a condemned man. Everything—my life, sanity, and reputation—seemed on the line. For a year now, I had driven myself to this point. I wanted to do it and I had to do it and I was terrified. Now it was time.

Outside it was still dark. On my way now, I moved through the morning's motions, so long anticipated but hardly real: rising from a pad in my bare apartment, to which I'd just moved; dressing in the clothes—a favorite flannel shirt, pants, and bandanna—that I'd set out the night before; heating up my breakfast—eggs and a piece of steak—which I washed down with a bit of water.

At five, as I was eating, Ron di Giovanni called. Ron is a friend and balloonist. On many flights, I've served as copilot, navigator, ground crew, Sherpa. Now, unasked, Ron had telephoned the control towers of several airports for weather reports, and I was touched. Thursday, May 26, 1977, promised to be a beautiful day, clear and warm with moderate winds. I was relieved to hear it. Had the weather been bad, the winds

THE WORLD TRADE
CENTER, AS SEEN
FROM THE EAST.

high, I would have had to postpone the climb. Not that this would have been a big production: the ascent was not a massive orchestration that had been set in motion and could be stopped only with difficulty. It wasn't D-day. It was just me. And my younger brother Stephen and my good friend Jery Hewitt, who would be driving me to the building.

A bit later, the telephone rang again. Jery calling to make sure I was up. Jery lived in Queens then, only a short distance from my apartment. The plan was for him to pick up Steve, who was staying with my parents, along the way. He was just leaving, he said. He'd be here in a few minutes.

Five-fifteen now, and it was starting to get light. The morning was very still, with only the sounds of the birds and an occasional passing car. I pulled a windbreaker over my shirt— it might be chilly up on the tower—and put on a large jacket over that, one that would be big enough to hide my climbing gear later. Then I gathered up my pack and a box filled with the equipment I'd be using, and I went downstairs to wait.

At five-thirty, Jery and Stephen pulled up—a little late, enough to make me restless; Steve had overslept. I piled my things in Jery's pickup, and we started driving toward the city. A tape of Jean Luc Ponte's music was playing on the cassette deck. "I thought you'd like to hear this," Jery said, turning to me.

"Nice," I said. "Thanks." In college, when everyone had been mad for rock, Jery and I had preferred jazz and blues. It was just one of the ways in which we liked to think we were different.

On the way, I busied myself putting on my climbing harness and shoes. "I just hope I'm not stopped," I said, mostly to myself. I was all nerves now, thinking of the climb. Already adrenaline was flowing; I could feel it. I was trembling.

As we crossed the Kosciusko Bridge on the Brooklyn-Queens Expressway, I saw the twin towers of the World Trade Center. The sun was starting to rise and the towers' silver corners stood out brightly, glinting in the light, and the rest of the buildings was dim and white, rising up and up far above everything around them. That silver glint from the corner I planned to climb was a magnet drawing me to it, and looking at it, I felt a surge of energy and goosebumps tingling on my skin, as if there had been an electrical connection between the building and me and my seeing it had caused a charge to flow between us. It was vast. It seemed impossible that later in the morning, *that* morning, I would actually be up there. This is it, I kept thinking. I couldn't wait to be up there and couldn't bear the element of chance that, however thorough my preparations, could prevent me from getting there.

Something else was worrying me. Stephen was to be married in two days, and the chances were good that I'd miss the ceremony. I felt terrible about it, and now, in the truck, I turned to him. "I'm sorry if I'm arrested and I can't be at your wedding," I told him. "I hope you won't be upset. It isn't that I don't care about being there. I just feel I have to do this now. I can't put it off." How could I explain?

"I understand," Steve said, smiling. "Don't worry about it." But I did.

At that hour of the morning there was little traffic. We breezed into the city, across the Brooklyn Bridge, through the Wall Street area, and over to the corner of Church and Dey streets, just east of the World Trade Center plaza, where we parked. I got out of the truck, feeling like a bomb ready to explode. Had someone tapped me on the shoulder, that alone might have detonated me. I was so worked up now that I thought I might have a nervous breakdown. It seemed possible I'd simply collapse, that Steve and Jery would have to drag me back into the truck and home. It was a level of excitement unparalleled in my experience, approached only by the first few times I went climbing.

Standing beside the pickup, I put my pack on and draped my jacket over it, as camouflage. However, this only had the effect of making the pack more conspicuous. I couldn't walk onto the plaza looking like Quasimodo in a cape and expect not to be noticed. Better to be disarmingly (I hoped) direct. I took both off, then put the jacket on and the pack over it. An improvement, but still too bulky. So I took it off again and kept rearranging the things inside the pack to make it appear smaller. At last I had it loaded in a way I found satisfactory, and we started walking across the street toward the plaza. All my gear — my climbing rope, devices, hooks, carabiners, and other paraphernalia — was hanging from my belt, clanging away as I climbed the steps; I felt like a walking bell tower. Why hadn't I called the police and *announced* what I planned to do?

But the plaza was deserted, as I hoped it would be. We strolled around, trying to appear nonchalant, tourists taking snapshots, as we checked for security guards. I stood looking up at the tower. "Do you see anybody?" I asked Steve quietly. "Do you see anybody around?"

"No," he said softly. "No one."

"All right." I walked over to the corner of the south tower. A little fence framed a small construction area near the corner, and I squeezed through the two-foot space between it and the building. Jery walked off toward the middle of the plaza, where he could get a better view of the different approaches. Moving quickly now, I knelt on the ground and got my things out. The evening before, I'd visited the plaza to install the portions of my climbing devices that fitted inside the channel — the feature of the building I'd exploit to make my ascent. The windows of the World Trade Center (as well as these of many other modern skyscrapers) are washed by machine. The cleaning mechanism, lowered from the top of the tower, automatically cleans the windows as it moves, then rises

CLIMBING DEVICE
ASSEMBLED IN THE
CHANNEL.

back up to the summit. These channels—there are two of them, forty inches apart on each corner of the building—are really tracks on which a scaffolding is lowered and raised. They stabilize it, preventing it from blowing around in the wind.

To my relief, the plates and bolts were still in the right-hand channel where I'd left them. As rapidly as I could, I screwed them to the housing of the devices, the part that fits outside the channel. These devices, designed to slide along this track, have only one moving part—a lever that from the outside resembles a hook. It rotates up and down. When the lever's outside end goes down, its inside end, a cam, rises up and presses against the outside of the channel, pinching it against the plate within. My weight, by means of a sling and a stirrup, would be on the lever; the more weight, the tighter the devices would squeeze the channel. Once my weight was off the lever, it could be raised. Then the cam would retract, and the device would slide freely in the channel. Or so I had designed it to work.

The channels themselves, made of stainless steel, are exceptionally strong. Five quarter-inch stainless screws attach each twelve-foot section of channel to the structure. Just one of those screws would probably hold a thousand pounds—more than seven times my weight. Their sheer strength—the amount of downward force they will sustain before snapping—is far greater than any strain I would impose on them. The channels had withstood several years of wear; I had no reason to suppose they'd come off now. Compared with the weight of the window-washing machine, my own, 160 pounds, was slight.

By this time, it was close to six-thirty. Though we were in the shade, the sun was shining brightly higher up on the tower, twenty or thirty stories above us. The sun turned the corner into a glimmering blade that divided the blue sky. Above me, the tower was impossibly, dizzyingly high: one quarter of a mile to the top, 1350 feet, 110 stories. It was time I got going.

Jery was off near the middle of the plaza, nervously looking around. Steve stayed close to me, taking pictures as I installed the devices. Suddenly, I heard him say, "*Somebody's coming!*"

My heart stopped.

"Who is he?" I asked. "What does he look like?" Did he, I meant, have a uniform? Did he look official?

"I don't know," Steve said. "A guy."

Still kneeling on the ground, I looked up and saw him. He was a middle-aged man wearing work clothes. At least he was not a cop.

"Hi!" I said, sitting back. "Howya doin'?"

"Okay," The man nodded. He kept on going. Apparently he didn't find it peculiar that I was sitting there at daybreak, staring at the corner of a building. Perhaps in New York this wasn't so odd after all.

"Phew!" I said. "Close call!"

"Yeah," said Steve.

A minute or two later, I had my two devices attached, one above the other, in the bottom of the channel. My stirrups, one for each foot, were connected to the devices, as was my harness. I was ready. Randy Zeidberg, the girl I'd been seeing more or less constantly for the past year, was supposed to have joined us and hadn't. I was disappointed, but I couldn't wait.

Trembling, I raised the top device as high as I could. I lifted my right foot and stepped up, putting my weight on the stirrup. The device locked. I was off the ground. As I stepped up, I slid the left device up underneath the right one. The stirrup leading to the bottom device was eighteen inches shorter than the one attached to the top instrument. Then I stepped up again, putting my weight this time on my left foot; the left device locked, and I was free to raise the right one higher. As I climbed, my weight was always on one foot or the other.

"Well, Steve," I said, "I'm on my way."

"Hey, those things work nice."

"Thanks," I said. Steve's wedding was still on my mind. "I'm sorry about the wedding," I told him again. "I hope I can make it."

Steve waved away my regrets. "Have a good climb," he said. "I hope I'll see you later."

Then I started moving up the building as quickly as I could. When I was about fifteen feet up, Randy arrived.

"I'm sorry I'm late!" she called. "I wanted to see you."

I paused, smiling, to look at her.

"Good luck!" she called. "Be careful! Have a good climb!"

I took off my pack and my large gray jacket and tossed the coat down to her. "I won't need this now," I called. I kept the light windbreaker on, as it was cool in the shade and breezy, and put on my pack over it. Then I noticed three security guards and a Port Authority policeman walking slowly across the plaza toward the building. They were looking up at me quizzically. They appeared unsure of what it was that I was doing. Perhaps I was a maintenance worker. Perhaps there was a ladder. They walked forward, watching me. Then, suddenly, they started running.

Probably the largest incongruity in all this, beyond the obvious one of scrambling up a skyscraper wall, was that far from having been born to the mountains and climbing I am a city boy, raised in Queens. The second of five children—I have three younger brothers and an older sister—I grew up in a close-knit, middle-class Catholic family. My father is a stereotyper who works mostly for the *Daily News*. Until I was three, we lived on farms—first in Ronkonkoma on Long Island, then in Millbrook, New York—that my father managed. When this living proved threadbare, my father reluctantly gave up farming and we moved back to the city, where he and my mother had grown up. He went to work as a millwright for his father installing printing machines, and in time this led him to become a printer. In the Bellrose section of Queens, we lived in a "colonial" row house, (all the rooms were in a row, as in a railroad flat) much like Archie Bunker's, set on a narrow plot of land on 254th Street. Then when I was twelve, we moved to a more spacious house, a cape (now the rooms were in quarters), on a larger lot two blocks away, where my parents still live.

All pretty conventional, yet my mother and father always seemed different to me from other parents. For one thing, they didn't socialize a lot; their focus was on the family. For another, they felt little need to conform. Years after all my friends' families had televisions, for example, my brothers and sister and I still weren't allowed one (when we began spending more time in friends' houses than our own, our parents finally gave in; they wanted us home—but they kept a tight rein on our viewing). Not that my parents were so strict; it was rather a matter of emphasis. As we were growing up, they put a premium on our doing things together. One project or another always seemed to be in progress. Before Christmas, we'd make our own tree decorations. If any alterations on the house had to be undertaken, my parents always did the work themselves, involving us along the way. They encouraged self-reliance and independence. Their influence was exerted mostly by example as I recall them rarely talking about such things. All the same, the influence was felt. As a teenager, I didn't smoke or drink. Being different, resisting peer pressure, gave me a lot of pleasure. I may have paid a certain price in never quite belonging, but to me it was a source of pride not distress. Strength of character was the thing. It seemed important to me to go my own way.

This spirit of independence carried over into other things. I never became afraid, as so many people seem to, of building, fixing, making things, taking on mechanical projects of all kinds. My father used to hand me down his old, *old* cars, for example, and I'd have to fix (and fix) them to keep them running. Some of what I needed to know he taught me, some of it I got from books, a lot of it I picked up through trial and error; but there was never any question that doing it myself

MY MOTHER WITH, *LEFT TO RIGHT*, MY SISTER TERRY AND BROTHERS STEPHEN AND PAUL, AND MY- SELF, AGE 6.

would be better, both cheaper and more satisfying, than paying someone else to do it for me—which I couldn't have afforded in any case.

So I'm perpetually amazed at the readiness with which people will surrender themselves to others' alleged expertise. Not everyone is a mechanical whiz, I realize, but most people have far more aptitude than they suspect. Maintaining the things we depend on and enjoy is simply not that hard. If people would look only a little beneath the surface, the mystery—one that mechanics and repairmen are happy to perpetuate — would be dispelled. People would be astounded at how much they could do for themselves, how much money they'd save, and how much satisfaction this sort of freedom from dependency on others would bring them. In my family, these things were givens.

Another given at the Willig house was religion. Attendance at church was taken for granted. To my parents, "the family that prays together stays together" was more than a catchy saying; it was close to a literal truth. Evenings—with my mother as prime mover—we'd say the rosary together, kneeling on the dining-room floor. Most of my education was conducted by nuns and priests. My parents didn't allow me to see movies proscribed by the *Tablet*, a Catholic paper. Sex was never mentioned at home; guilt, following the normal pattern for this kind of upbringing, became the flip side of anything to do with sex. In my first amazed encounter with a girl, at least every *other* thought was for the confessional. Conscience became my sidekick. If I stole, my conscience always (if sometimes a little tardily) made me take the things back, sometimes riskier than the original larceny. These days, although I've become detached from formal Catholicism, I consider myself religious. Spiritual concerns are still on my mind.

I was shy, growing up, and acutely self-conscious. I went to a coed parochial school—green gabardine pants, white shirts, green ties, and strict nuns—and later to a public high school. While I had confidence in some areas, dealing with people wasn't one of them. Girls in particular paralyzed me, especially, of course, the ones I liked. In their presence, my imagined inadequacies would loom around me like balloons in the Macy's Thanksgiving day parade. With five children in the family, however, I never lacked companions. (For a long while, actually, there were six of us; when I was seven my mother found a one-and-a-half-year-old girl wandering, tattered and dirty, on our block. She took her in, scrubbed her clean, and the little girl, Nancy Belmonte, wound up staying with us for ten years. Nancy's mother was unwilling to care for her then; later, she remarried and insisted on taking Nancy back. Until recently, a Vietnamese girl lived with my parents. Christian values, my parents' gestures made clear, were to be put into

practice, not just mouthed on Sundays.) And I had
neighborhood friends I used to pal around with. But I was
always something of a loner, a role I valued then as a romantic
ideal (more on this later). In school, I was never quite in with
the supposed elite, yet not quite out either; accurately or not, I
felt my place among the right crowd was more tolerated than
assured. Ordinarily, I mixed little with my classmates; when
school was over I'd come right home.

In fact, I disliked almost everything about school. When I
was a little boy, I remember, I'd sometimes roll in puddles
during rain storms to establish a basis for the sicknesses I
planned to feign (under the eyes of a skeptical knowing mother,
I could never quite pull off these hoaxes.) I was an indifferent
student. Unlike my younger brother Paul or my father, who
often races through a book a day, I wasn't a natural reader.
Studying was an agony. I had a terrible time knuckling down
and seemed to have no ability at all to force myself. Facts
slipped right through me, like water through chicken wire.
Occasionally, I found a teacher's enthusiasm for a subject
infectious, but otherwise I was lost. In high school, I excelled in
only machine shop and drafting; I was good with my hands and
visual concepts but lacked the persistence for a subject.like
physics. It wasn't until college that I settled down.

As a kid, I was unusually easygoing and unassertive, I
suppose; for that reason, and because schoolboy bravado
always seemed idiotic to me, I've never been in a fistfight, not
even a boyhood scrap. The closest I ever came was in high
school, when a guy much larger than I became incensed that I
was seeing his girl friend—or rather former girl friend, a
change of which she had yet to persuade him. *I* was the
problem, he was sure. (An unlikely, if flattering, role for me.
She was entirely the aggressor, *years* ahead of me in this
department: I was incapable of moving in on anybody.) In any
case, Frank's idea of a solution was to come up to me in school,
snarl something about keeping away from *his* girl, and unload
a punch to my jaw. My head snapped to the side and back, I
slammed against a bank of lockers, then I silently turned
around and looked at him. No other reaction—I was too
surprised. And that was the end of it. Or not quite. Apparently
my stalwart routine unnerved Tom. From others I heard that
he'd become convinced that such impassivity without must
surely mean fires within. It was only a matter of time before I'd
whale the living daylights out of him. A !ew days later, he came
up to me, all hail remorse. "Hey, George, listen—the other day
I got a little carried away. No hard feelings, huh?" So the
mysterious stare, I learned, could be mightier than the fist. A
short while later, the girl became bored with me, too. As I said,
I was out of my league.

Another way in which I was atypical as a boy was my total
lack of interest in competitive sports. Baseball, football, and
basketball may be national obsessions, but they certainly

WITH MY FATHER
AND BROTHERS,
STEPHEN *(LEFT)* AND
PAUL, ON THE DAY OF
MY FIRST COMMUN-
ION. SHORTLY AFTER
THIS PICTURE WAS
TAKEN I SPILLED
GRAPE SODA ON MY
NEW WHITE JACKET.

weren't—and aren't—mine. Un-American as it seems, I've never been to a professional ballgame of any kind—basket, foot, or base. Aside from a couple of climbing journals, I don't read any sports magazines or news. I've never cared what happens in the bullpen.

My few brushes with the sport that most boys grow up breathing were hardly likely to kindle a fever in me for the game.

First episode. At age five, I was trying with much embarrassment to play baseball with a neighborhood boy who was a year older. Ralph, the heavy in this story, was maliciously needling me with every missed pitch. "Man, you *stink*," he kept saying. "You're really bad." The harder I tried, the less happened. Eye, hand, and bat were just not cooperating. Finally, probably accidentally, I did connect, but the results weren't happy. My hit opened a crack in the bat— Ralph's, naturally—which closed on my hand. A stab of pain raced up my arm. "I don't want play any more," I managed to snuffle sensibly, then dropped the dratted bat and went inside. That's the last time I picked up a baseball bat.

Second (and final) episode. This one was no more promising. Now in the third grade, and on my way back to school after lunch, I was walking through a cinder lot where some boys were playing ball. One of them hit a fly; as if directed by crabby fortune, it came winging toward *me*. The sun was (naturally) shining right in my eyes. This made no real difference; even in the best of circumstances, I knew no more about catching a ball than I did about swinging a bat. I didn't know how to gauge its trajectory, didn't know when to close my hands. All the same, I tried to time it, reached out my hands . . . and the ball landed squarely on my forehead. *Bong.* Stunned (but somehow not surprised), I went wobbling away. Needless to say, another turnoff.

The only sport I've ever competed in was swimming, and that was back in grammar school. My racing career was short-lived. The problem was, I *hated* the competition. So much so that, at some meets, I just couldn't go through with it. I'd be churning along, ahead of the pack, and I'd simply ... stop. To me, it was far more than a race. It was a great traumatic drama. The judgment of other people was on me, I thought. My worth as a person, in their eyes, seemed to hinge on how well I swam. If I lost, my value seemed in question. Winning gave me no greater pleasure. I couldn't shake the awareness that someone *else* was losing, and I could identify all too closely with the way he felt. I was obviously intense as a kid and took it all very, very seriously—probably too seriously. Eventually the competition became intolerable to me, and I quit.

Competition ruins sports for many kids, of course. By now, the horror that Little League "play" can be is well documented. Happily, my parents didn't push me. Some temperaments may thrive on competition, but mine wasn't one of them. I didn't see the point. My satisfaction lay elsewhere.

I liked to build things, to fashion little worlds. A paint-mixing stick became a surfboard. I used to make little tikis, Polynesian figurines, as I dreamed of the South Seas. Over a period of years, I constructed a mammoth railroad that filled my whole room, hungrily spreading everywhere but in the small space occupied by my bed. By the time I was fourteen, it was getting so big and involved so much work that I became frightened; I started envisioning myself up there for years working on it. Man, I thought, I'd better dismantle this thing; its's taking me over. With relief, I disassembled it one day and threw out the wood. At that time, building things gave me such satisfaction that I thought I might like to be an engineer or architect.

Much as I enjoyed such solitary pursuits, they were only part of the picture. My brothers and I used to play games all the time: cops and robbers—team ring-a-lievo on bicycles at night over perhaps a ten-block area, even through distant neighbors' backyards, which were hidden lands pervaled with the peril of double discovery; hide-and-seek for hours, all through the house (this one I played into my twenties; my favorite hiding place was at the very top of a closet, just beneath the ceiling, where I'd wedge myself between the walls like a telescoping chinning bar and wait); rubber-band battles that used to go on for days, even at the dinner table when my parents weren't looking. When we moved to the larger house in Bellrose, my parents had a second story added but left the upstairs, where my brothers and I lived, unfinished. Instead of walls, there were frames of two-by-fours. Although we had our separate rooms, we could of course see through where the walls were supposed to be. It was like living on a stage set. It fired the imagination. We used to have marathon sessions of Risk and Monopoly up there, playing for days and days through beautiful weekends. We all collected stamps too. With so much company and activity, I rarely lacked diversion.

Most of all, though, as I was growing up I loved the outdoors and remote, unspoiled places. To be away from the buildings, congestion, and other people. First in the Boy Scouts and later in the Explorers, I went hiking and camping whenever I could. I loved swimming and body surfing, particularly when the waves were very large and would hurl you forward, ahead of the curl, as if shot from a cannon. Sometimes I'd spend four hours straight at it, never leaving the water.

Summers we'd go to the beach or visit relatives. One aunt lived in Howard Beach, near Kennedy Airport, where she had a house on stilts over the water. I'd spend my days there with my cousin Harry paddling around in his dingy, crabbing and fishing. Another aunt lived out on Long Island near Huntington, an area that at the time was still woodland and farms. As a small boy, I used to look forward to these visits for weeks. On our drives out there—or anywhere in the country for that matter—I would sit behind my father, lean over the seatback and look out the window. My mother, brothers, and sister would sing songs together as we drove— "Old Macdonald Had a Farm," and the like—but I had no urge to join in. I just wanted to look out at the trees and passing scenery and dream.

Adventure and exploration filled my fantasies. I wanted to sail a two-master schooner in the South Pacific (no coincidence that my favorite television show was *Adventures in Paradise*), dive for treasure in the Caribbean, explore the rain forests of South America. My childhood heroes weren't athletes. They were explorers like Thor Heyerdahl, who did exciting, adventurous things. Individualistic people who left their cultures and became, for a time, islands in another. My fascination with the tropics led me to an interest in plants, especially palms, which seemed to bring me a little closer to the places I yearned to visit.

When I was seven, an uncle showed me slides of a trip through the American west, and I saw for the first time pictures of the Grand Canyon, the deserts of Arizona, and the great mountains. From then on, these places filled my thoughts, and my uncle became a role model: he was a bachelor; he had his own business; he traveled as he pleased. I didn't want to marry, to be tied down by a family. I didn't want to be dependent on anyone. The outward push of the city, the disappearance of the woods, had filled me from the time I was a small child with a distaste for people and the trappings they brought with them. I would be on my own. Alone. Away from the crowds. To a romantic, suggestible disposition, it seemed like the ideal life. Then.

BAXTER'S PINNACLE IN THE GRAND TETONS. I'M ON THE LEFT.

The security guards and Port Authority policeman were at the base of the building, confronting Randy, Jery, and Stephen.

"What's going on?" I heard one of them ask. "*What are you doing?*" he called up to me.

Push. Using the heel of my hand, I slid the top device as high as I could reach and stepped up.

"I'm climbing the building." I did not look down.

"Come down here right now," the policeman snapped.

In one motion, I raised the bottom device until it was just beneath the top one and stepped up with my left foot. Now the sling attached to the top device and to my right foot was slack again.

"*Get down here.*"

"Nope," I called, "I can't. These devices only work one way." Untrue, of course. I could have come down, but I had no intention of doing it.

"*Get down here. Now.*"

Push. The device slid into the channel, and I continued to climb. Twenty feet up now, I began to shake so badly that I had to stop. For a moment, I even considered going down. Refusing to comply with a police officer seemed an enormous thing to be doing. This symbol of authority carried a surprising amount of weight. Everything American — Mom, apple pie, Uncle Sam, the flag, the whole corny works — seemed to converge in that blue uniform, and here for the first time in my life I was flagrantly, calculatedly defying it. This wasn't the kind of thing that people got away with. Taking deep breaths, I tried to calm down. "Protect me, God," I began to pray. "Help me to do this, I really want to do this. It just means so much to me. Don't let anyone get hurt. I want everything to be okay." Finally, when I was a little more composed I looked down at the cop. "The only way to go from here," I said, "is up." Sliding the top device up the channel, I started climbing again.

"*I said get the fuck down here, you asshole!*"

Raising the bottom device, I stepped up another foot and a half. Moving from side to side, I was trying to coordinate the two motions of lifting and stepping to make them as fluid as possible. In the act of stepping up onto the top device, I tried to use my left hand to raise the bottom one; as I stepped onto the bottom device, I tried to raise the top one. In this way, the climbing would become one continuous motion, like ascending a ladder.

"You're going to kill yourself! You're fucking crazy!"

Thirty feet now. Eyes to the track, I kept going.

He tried another ploy. "Those channels don't go all the way to the top of the building. You're gonna get killed!" Cagey, but of course I knew better, having surveyed the corners of the tower with binoculars.

"Nope," I called, "I'm going up." From that point on, I didn't answer as he continued shrieking. I tried to ignore him and

AT THE START OF THE CLIMB.

concentrate on the task at hand. It wasn't easy, as he was quite beside himself now, jumping around, actually jumping up and down, screaming crazily at me. All appeals to reason were forgotten in his mixture of invective and helpless rage. "Get down from there! I said get down! Get down here, youstupidasshole, get down from there!" His voice was cracking, going hoarse, growing fainter as I climbed. Glancing down, I saw that several other policemen had joined him. Jery, Stephen, and Randy were looking up at me worriedly. Frankly I was worried, too. What I was doing, given the cop's reaction, seemed all the more extreme. Vague thoughts of getting in trouble no longer seemed hypothetical. It was too late, though; too much had gone into it. I wasn't about to stop.

"Take off! Get out of here!" I called down to Randy and the others. Uselessly—they had already been taken into custody. After that, for a long while I did not look down.

Just now, I had other things to think about. For this part of the climb I had a plan, and it was crucial that I let nothing distract me. As quickly as possible, I had to get up one hundred feet, ten stories, beyond which point the fire department's longest ladder could not reach. Above that height, it would be very difficult for the firemen to intercept me. Even though I suspected they'd be unable to mobilize, position, and brace a truck in time to grab me, I couldn't take any chances; a fire station was only two blocks away. And so I climbed, pushing hard, trying to shut out everything but the drive to go up and up.

On the plaza, four eight-story buildings are clustered beside the two towers. My first goal was to get even with the tops of these. This would open up my view and offer a reassuring sign of progress: I would be more than halfway to safety.

At fifty feet now, I was almost there. I was breathing heavily from both the exertion and my agitation. My heart was pounding. A couple of times, the thought that I should go down intruded, but I swatted it away impatiently and kept climbing.

Down below, the policeman had stopped screaming, probably from exhaustion. From blocks away, the sirens were shrieking, multiplying, converging, continuing to come, one after the other. It seemed remarkable that they should be coming for me. Well, now I'm an outlaw, I thought. A criminal. I've got to do the best I can. No more doubts entered my mind. Nothing beyond reaching the hundred-foot mark. The dogs were at my heels. This was my only chance. I was scared, very scared. I felt like a fugitive running for his life, crashing through the brush.

All those sirens. Kojak, I thought. Kojak's coming, too.

CIRCLE SHOWS WHERE THE B-25 CRASHED INTO THE EMPIRE STATE BUILDING.

MY MOTHER RECEIV-ING FIRST AID AFTER THE CRASH.

WITH MY FATHER AND TERRY ON THE OBSERVATION DECK OF THE EMPIRE STATE BUILDING.

Strangely enough, one of my earliest memories as a small boy, of a visit with my parents to the top of the Empire State Building, centers around a fear of heights. My family history has been curiously entwined with celebrated skyscrapers; when, in July 1945, a twin-engine B-25 army bomber crashed into the seventy-ninth floor of the Empire State Building, my mother, a nineteen-year-old secretary for the Catholic Relief War Services, was one of those working on that floor. Eleven people in her office were killed; seven others, including my mother, were injured but survived. Fewer than ten years later we were all on the building's observation deck. My father sat me on the ledge, where I could see over the edge. A large plate of glass protected me from falling, and beyond this there was a railing with sharp metal jaws. All the same, looking down terrified me, and I clung closely to my father.

Not the most promising beginning for a climber, but my fear of height must have soon left me, for by the time I was six I was climbing a tall maple tree in front of my parents' house in Bellrose. I was the only kid in the neighborhood who was able to do it. The tree had a high, straight trunk, too wide to get my arms around. But by bearhugging it with my hands and feet I could shinny up until I reached the limbs. Then I would clamber up until the branches began swaying and tipping, perhaps forty feet above the ground. The first time I climbed the tree, I remember my mother and sister looking up anxiously at me calling, "Come on down!" Come down? A new world had opened up. An island with a satisfying gulf that separated me from everyone else. The tree was a fine place to get away to and be alone. "No, I'm okay," I called. I preferred to stay up there, winging around with the breeze.

From that time on I climbed, not voraciously but simply attempting things—trees as a boy and later rocks and cliffs when they caught my notice and seemed appealing. In the Explorers, which I'd joined in my teens as a way of going hiking and camping, I become known as the Human Fly or Mountain Goat. My first high climb was of a cliff alongside a waterfall in the Catskills during an Explorer outing. The rock was wet, about two hundred feet from the ground to the top of the falls. Using no technical aids (which I knew nothing about then in any case), my brother Paul and I climbed the cliff taking pictures along the way. While it wasn't difficult by the standards of what I'd be doing later, it was certainly exciting at the time.

Not long afterward, I began climbing structures. To visit a girl friend at State University at Farmingdale, I'd climb to her third-story window (particularly after men's parietals) working my way up between two fluted extensions on the building's facade. The women's dorms at C. W. Post proved no less accessible (from the outside). A friend's colonial-style house provided another impromptu climb—up the front, over

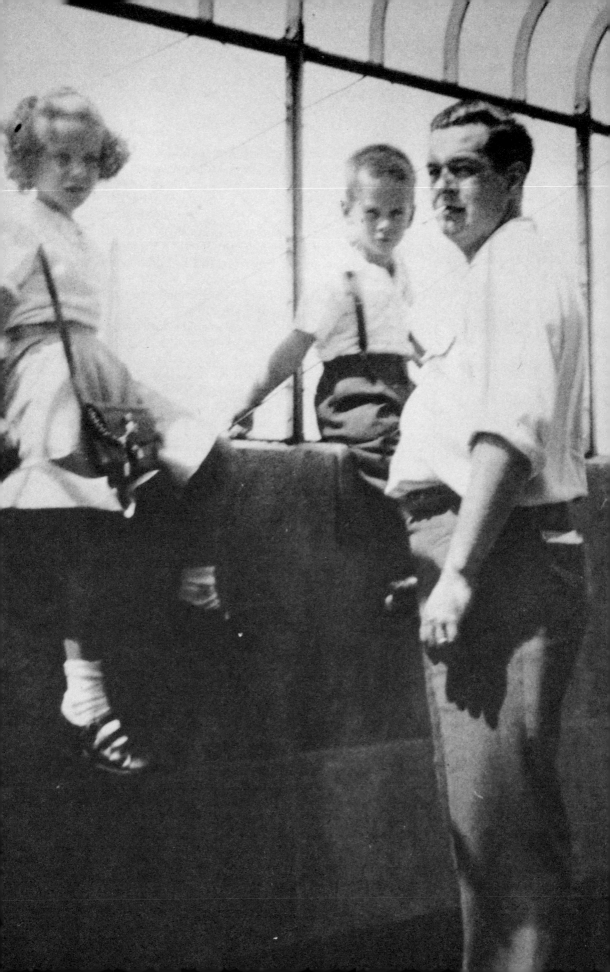

the roof, and down the back. Then when I was twenty, a concert at the Singer Bowl in Flushing Meadows Park (Jimi Hendrix, Janis Joplin, and the Chambers Brothers were performing) presented a fortification (this is the way I regarded structures, as citadels to be invaded) that was considerably more challenging. It was always a temptation to sneak into these summertime outdoor rock concerts. Thousands of people without tickets would mill around outside, where the faint sounds of the music and the crowd within could be heard. Occasionally, a group of kids would storm the gates, and some of them would even make it through. It was a wild and festive atmosphere. To me, the music was secondary; the real attraction was the challenge of devising a way to penetrate the security.

And so on this evening I strolled around, looking for a weakness in the stadium's system. Then I noticed it: a light pole, three feet away from a one-story extension from the stadium (which was itself a cone, broad end up). After shinnying up this pole quickly, I jumped onto the extension's roof. Then, using a beam, I climbed up the side of the stadium; its wall pitched obliquely toward me, so that as I was climbing I was almost upside down. Finally I came up over the edge; the people in the last row turned around in astonishment.

"Holy shit!" they exclaimed. "What the hell! How'd you do it?"

"I just climbed up," I said.

"Great!" they said. People were laughing, coming over to shake my hand.

After this climb, what could the concert offer? Now I felt like *climbing*. "Well," I announced during a boring interlude, "I'm gonna go back down and get an orange drink." Showboating, I admit. Retracing my steps, I climbed down, made my purchase, and clambered back up again carrying a drink for someone else in my teeth. The upper rim of the stadium was maybe fifty feet high, the technical equivalent of an overhang. It was the first high, difficult climbing that I did.

Bitten by the bug, I also climbed into concerts at the New York State Pavilion, also in Flushing Meadows Park on the grounds of the 1964 World's Fair. I could easily have bought a ticket, of course, but it wouldn't have been nearly as much fun. Once again, I began by walking around, searching for a point of weakness. It didn't take long to spot one. Pillars, I noticed, supported a roof suspended above the structure. Using a technique climbers call "chimneying" (although I didn't know it then), I pressed my back against one of these pillars, my feet and hands against the main structure, and shimmied up in the gap between them. This was a relatively easy way to get in, however, and others were using it too; not long afterward, security people greased the pillars to discourage it.

A setback, but soon I spotted another way in. On the outside wall of the building there was a doorway, a service entrance that did not appear to be in use. This door became my ticket. Standing on its lower hinge, I would step up onto the doorknob, from which point I could just reach a small vent on the side of the building. Pulling myself up by this vent, I would step onto the upper hinge; then I could reach the guardrail and pull myself over. It was only a matter of climbing fifteen feet. A couple of years ago, showing a friend some of my earlier climbs, I tried that door again; still a piece of cake, I can report, should the ticket booth be less than obliging.

MY BROTHER STE-
PHEN, MOVING UP A
CHIMNEY

I t was mayhem down on the street. Every so often I'd pause to look. No fire engines in sight yet, but police cars kept arriving, one after another, their sirens wailing. Energy seemed to be flowing all around the city. A knot of people stood looking up at me. The police were making no further effort to communicate with me. What could they say?

Moving steadily, hungry for quick advance, I was powering up the building, hot and sweaty now, still intent on reaching that hundred-foot mark. My concentration was so focused on the progress of my ascent that I was in something close to a meditative state.

My hands were beginning to hurt from hitting the devices. No problem with their holding me: the instruments' locking action was so effective that I had to smack them with the heel of my hand to get them moving again in the channel. This wasn't the only problem; channels that from a distance appeared to be razor-straight close-up actually wavered here and there out of line. The aluminum panels on the building's corner, which seen from below seemed to form a mirrorlike, slickly impervious surface, in fact curved erratically in and out. As a result, from panel to panel the channels were slightly out of alignment, with about a quarter inch of space separating them. Using my hand, I had to hammer the devices to force them through these junctures. With nearly each step, either because of the device's locking action or the irregularity of the joints, it was necessary to give the instruments a curt, forceful smack. This was taking its toll on my hands.

As I climbed, I darted nervous looks around, trying to gauge my progress by adjacent buildings. At last, even with a margin for safety, I figured I had it: one hundred feet. Beyond which no ladder would reach. For the moment at least, I was safe. (Later I'd learn that fire trucks hadn't been allowed on the plaza because World Trade Center authorities feared their heavy tires might damage the valuable tiles.) I'd expended a tremendous amount of energy scampering up so quickly, and now I was getting tired. I leaned back to rest. With my harness attached to the devices, I could sit back comfortably, with my arms free. Now I was alone with only the tower above me. The crowd below was still small.

CLIMBING A VERTI-
CAL ICE WALL USING
ICE TOOLS.

ICE CLIMBING NEAR
KAATERSKILL FALLS
IN THE CATSKILLS.

During the period when I was devising ways into stadiums, climbing played no big part in my life. Up to this point I'd spent as much time outdoors as I could, hiking and camping, and I climbed whatever came along whenever it seemed possible. But these climbs were really nothing more than occasional escapades. My total knowledge of rock climbing then was the little I'd seen in Disney's *First Man on the Mountain*. I hadn't thought about technical climbing; I knew nothing about it. The idea was as foreign and unavailable to me as going out in space. When I was twenty-three, however, I saw something that changed this.

On a December evening in 1972, quite by accident I saw a short about climbing, called *Solo*, made by a photographer named Mike Hoover; it was playing along with Woody Allen's *Everything You Always Wanted to Know About Sex...*, which I had gone to see. *Solo* was about a man scaling a massive cliff alone. It was electrifying. In one sequence, the climber was hanging, a couple of *thousand* feet up, underneath a roof—a horizontal overhang. Suspended from slings, in turn connected to pitons—metal spikes with holes at the end used as anchors in a rock—he was working his way along an overhead crack hammering in more pitons, when one pulled out. Like a shot, the climber dropped, swinging out over the dizzying space beneath the overhang and held by another piece of protection in the crack. Later, another piton fell, and the camera followed it as it careened down, clattering against the side of the giant wall for what seemed like minutes before it reached the bottom: it wasn't hard to imagine what would happen to a climber should his equipment fail.

Shortly afterward, as we held our breath, the man did a dramatic climbing move called a "pendulum": suspended, still thousands of feet up, from a piece of protection higher on the wall, he swung Tarzan-like on his rope way across the rock face to reach another crack system. A helicopter shot at the end of the film showed the climber standing at the summit of the wall, having done what he set out to do, balancing precariously in the wind. *Never* had I seen a group of people so mesmerized by something as that audience was by *Solo*. My skin tingled as I watched. From that moment on, I knew that climbing was for me. *Solo* was simply the most exciting, the most uplifting, thing I had ever seen. It changed my life.

As I left the theater, I turned to the friends I was with and said, "That's it. That's what I want to do." It was absolutely clear to me, as things seldom are. For days afterward, I talked about the film.

At the time, I was working as a maker of prototypes for a Long Island medical equipment company called Ark Research. Employees there were given a day off for Christmas shopping; shortly after seeing *Solo*, I used this holiday to go into Manhattan in search of lightweight rain parkas, useful in

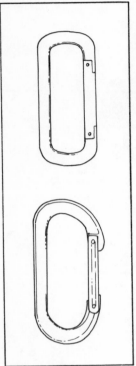

CARABINERS.

CRAMPONS.

backpacking, for my brothers. One store I visited, Kreeger and Son, also happened to carry climbing equipment. Delighted, I spent hours there poring over the paraphernalia. Finally, I purchased a book called *Bergsteigen* (a German word meaning "rock climbing"); another titled *Basic Rock Craft*, a classic by Royal Robbins, a celebrated California climber; and a couple of magazines. Back at home that evening, I devoured them, absorbing the lore, studying the principles and techniques, coveting the equipment, and thrilling to the photographs of climbers in "extreme" (a word climbers use that means highly exposed and vulnerable) positions. I learned a good deal.

Soon afterward, I found out about another climbing shop in Scarsdale, New York, called Alpine Recreation and made a number of visits there within a brief period. My ostensible purpose was Christmas shopping (and I did buy small gifts—heavy socks, warm woolen mittens, various articles of outdoor equipment), but really what I was doing was becoming steeped in the trappings of climbing. Equipment hung in rack after rack along the walls there, a world waiting in readiness that I couldn't wait to explore. Then someone at Alpine Recreation happened to mention still another climbing store, Eastern Mountain Sports, a chain with an outlet in Ardsley, New York, and I drove over there. EMS, I learned, ran a school in North Conway, New Hampshire, in the White Mountains, where during the winter ice-climbing seminars were offered. I couldn't wait. That evening I asked my brother Stephen if he'd be interested in joining me; he agreed, and I made reservations for ice-climbing lessons on the first available weekend

On a Friday night in February 1973, Steve and I drove up to North Conway in a heavy rain. We spent the night in the parking lot outside the EMS shop in my van, a four-wheel-drive Dodge Power wagon with oversized tires; I used to take it out onto the beach on Fire Island to get away and experience the ocean wilderness. I'd rigged an air compressor in it to inflate inner tubes, which I joined together for white water rafting trips in the fast rivers of the Catskills. Now I had no thoughts for anything but climbing. In the morning, Steve and I presented ourselves to our instructor, Hugh Thompson, who was an EMS guide in his mid-twenties. From stock in the store, he outfitted us with the equipment we'd be using that day: crampons—sharp metal claws that are attached to one's boots; helmets; and swami belts—one-inch nylon webbing wound around the waist to which rope is attached. The swami belt and the rope provide the basis for a climber's security in a fall. Hugh also gave us ice axes. These have three sharp points: a scooplike adze on one end, used for chopping steps in the ice; a narrower longer pick with teeth on the other end used for digging in and holding; and a spike at the base of the metal handle that is used for support, as a walking stick might be.

Ordinarily in ice climbing, one also employs an ice hammer—a smaller ax-like instrument—so that between the hands and feet there are four points of security: two crampons and two axes, three of which would be in the ice at any given time. On this first day, however, we wouldn't be climbing anything steep enough to require a hammer. In addition, Hugh selected some ice screws—ring-topped threaded spikes that, as their name suggests, are actually screwed into the ice for protection. And, last, we were given a strong 150-foot nylon rope, slings, and assorted carabiners—metal rings, either oval or D-shaped, with spring-loaded gates, used to connect different pieces of climbing equipment (an ice screw and the rope, for example).

We loaded all this into my truck and drove a couple of miles out of town, where we parked. Then we hiked through two-foot-deep snow up a hillside, down some railroad tracks, and up to a forty-five or fifty degree treeless slope. This was Willie Slide, where we would be climbing. It was mild now, around or just above freezing, and misting in a fine steady drizzle. Because of the mist, I couldn't see the mountains on the other side of the valley.

Seepage from springs on top of Willie Slide had fallen and frozen, forming what is technically known as "water ice" (as opposed to "glacier ice," which is composed of congealed snow). The ice was hard, a couple of feet thick, and slabby; because the seepage had been gradual, the ice had formed in layers. It was near white in color, shading toward blue, translucent, at points clouded by the air that had dispersed in it. Beneath the ice was rock. I looked up at the slope; an avalanche had left it clear and bald. It didn't look bad to me.

Standing at the bottom, Hugh showed us how to wind our swami belts around our waists, how to secure the webbing with a water knot (or ring knot, as it is sometimes called), and how to tie into the rope. He explained the belay system to us—the means by which one person protects another with the rope that joins them. Certain signals are used when climbing, he told us. A climber calls "on belay" when he is tied in, safely secured to a position, and ready to begin providing protection to another climber; "off belay" when the protection is no longer necessary (when, for example, the climber has reached a ledge to which he has secured himself); "belay off" when the belayer has dismantled his belay position; and "climbing" when the climber begins ascending. While one person belays, the leader (the first one up the route) climbs, placing protection (ice screws that will break and shorten a fall) as he proceeds until he has climbed a rope length (called a "pitch") or found a convenient position, usually a ledge, where he can tie in and begin belaying another climber. This sequence is repeated until the climbers complete their ascent. The last climber, the follower, "cleans" the pitch by removing the protection as he goes.

Next Hugh showed us how ice screws work and demonstrated different techniques of moving on ice.

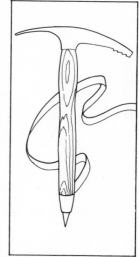

ICE AX.

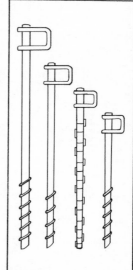

ICE SCREWS.

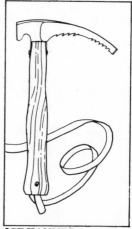

ICE HAMMER.

Crampons have ten sharp points that angle down and two that stick straight out front. In the "front-pointing" method, a climber kicks these two front teeth into the ice and walks up as if he were climbing a ladder. In the French system, a climber uses only the crampon's bottom teeth. Instead of moving straight up the slope, he zigzags, moving diagonally up in one direction and then reversing it. As he climbs, the bottom points of the crampon are flat against the ice and the ankle is bent at an angle that depends upon the steepness of the slope. If the steepness isn't severe, the French system is less strenuous than the front-pointing method, which is hard on the calves.

Finally, we learned how to use an ice ax: how to hold it when walking up a slope; how to chop steps with the adze; and how, with steepening ice, to use the pick. Hugh also showed us how to "self-arrest," or stop ourselves in a slide by digging in the pick end of the ax. Steve and I practiced this until we could perform it to his satisfaction, and then we set off.

Hugh led while one of us belayed him. Along the way he explained what he was doing: where he would use the pick, and why; what the basis was for any given move. As we climbed, it continued to drizzle. Slabs of ice were breaking away. Occasionally, we had to step aside as hunks tumbled by us. At long last, here was the thing itself. We were on *ice*, pitched sheets of slippery ice, wearing crampons and helmets, wielding ice axes, working our way slowly up, roped together, *climbing*. We did one ascent, perhaps two hundred feet high; then after lunch we completed another slightly steeper one; and all too quickly the day was over. Unfortunately, at thirty dollars each we couldn't afford another. Tired, delighted, excited, we drove home to Queens.

Now I couldn't wait to go rock climbing. A month or so later, from a guy who worked at Alpine Recreation—I was still stopping by there to study the equipment—I learned about a guide named Dick Dumais. He gave me Dick's number and told me about the climbing area where Dick taught: the Schawangunks, near New Paltz, New York. A long, dramatic ridge of cliffs offering hundreds of different ascents, the Gunks, as it's commonly known, is highly celebrated in climbing circles. The area is rich in prized horizontal cracks and interesting overhangs; its cliffs are composed of a very hard, durable, and thus safe quartz conglomerate. The Gunks offers some of the most varied terrain of any climbing area in the world. In following years, I would spend scores of weekends there.

I called Dick right away and set a date, a couple of weeks later, on which Stephen and I would meet him at Rock and Snow, a climbing shop in New Paltz. In early March, we drove up there. Once again, we were outfitted with equipment and then rode with Dick to the climbing area. As we passed through the rolling farmland, we got our first view of the Gunks. At first sight, it is always a little startling: an apparently sheer rock wall, miles long and three hundred feet high, that seems to come out of nowhere and go on forever. At its base is an old carriage road from which all the climbs are accessible and where climbers gather to talk. Down there, Dick began to instruct us in the use of the equipment.

First he showed us how to handle the ropes and tie the commonly used knots. He taught us how to place nuts or chocks (small pieces of metal in a variety of sizes and shapes), which are wedged into cracks to hold ropes and thus provide a climber with protection.

Cracks in rock are almost always uneven. A climber places a nut in a wide space, pulls it down, and wedges it in; where the crack narrows, the nut will stay until he frees it. Unlike pitons, which are pounded into the cracks, nuts are usually easily removable and do not harm the rock. (Gradually during the last two decades and then more rapidly in the past few years, such celebrated climbers as Yvon Chouinard and John Stannard have become passionate converts to the "clean-climbing" method, in which the rock face is left unaltered, and nuts have come to eclipse pitons.) Nuts are now considered to be a much purer means of protection, affording a less artificial relationship with the rock.

In certain situations, pitons have to be used or a face can't be climbed, but these situations are comparatively rare and most climbers now regard pitons as a last resort. In hundreds of climbs at the Gunks, I've never had to drive a piton into the rock. At the time of this lesson, my reading had already made me contemptuous of the use of pitons (with the unshakable conviction of someone who'd never done a technical rock climb). Dick, I discovered, was more casual about it. He seemed to be a nice person, anyway.

After we'd practiced placing nuts, Dick coached us in belaying techniques for rock. What was particularly important, he stressed, was anchoring the rope securely on the belay ledge. The rope could pass around a boulder which would then become a belay point. Or you might tie into a tree. Or if there was a good crack available, a nut or a combination of nuts might be used as an anchor. Whatever the case, the idea in belaying is to attach yourself to some absolutely secure fixed point and then to position yourself so that, if the climber falls, his weight won't pull you off the ledge.

Now Dick took us up on some low-angled terrain, perhaps forty-five degrees, an inclination at which we could get the basics down without freaking out at the exposure. Along the way, he explained how and where he was placing the protection so that it would catch any fall. In principle, he said, you place the protection as high as possible, ideally above you, to minimize the length of any tumble; the lower the protection, the farther you'll fall. As he guided us, he also told us about basic climbing techniques.

The idea, he said, is to use the legs, which contain the

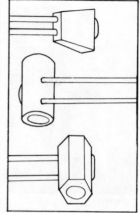

FROM TOP: WEDGE-SHAPED, TUBE, AND HEXAGONAL NUTS.

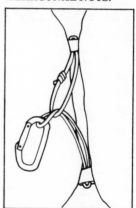

WEDGE-SHAPED NUTS, ANCHORED IN A VERTICAL CRACK.

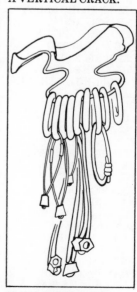

SLING WITH CARAB-INERS AND NUTS.

SURMOUNTING AN
OVERHANG AT THE
GUNKS.

FACING PAGE: *ABOVE*,
THE BOTTOM CLIMB-
ER, ANCHORED SEC-
URELY TO HIS BELAY-
ING POSITION, IS
FEEDING ROPE TO
THE ASCENDING
CLIMBER. NOTE HOW
THE ROPE PASSES
THROUGH THE THREE
CARABINERS SE-
CURED IN SLINGS TO
THE POINTS OF PRO-
TECTION—NUTS OR
PITONS—THAT THE
CLIMBER HAS PUT IN
EN ROUTE. *BELOW*,
THE BOTTOM
CLIMBER HAS
HALTED THE
LEADER'S FALL. SO
LONG AS THE BELAY-
ER HOLDS THE ROPE,
THE CLIMBER CAN
DROP NO FARTHER
THAN TWICE THE
DISTANCE HE WAS
FROM HIS LAST POINT
OF PROTECTION.

strongest muscles in the body, and the feet to do the work whenever possible. Hands are used primarily for balance and stability. While it is common for beginning climbers to try to pull themselves up with their hands, it is a mistake: hands are designed primarily for manipulation, and arms rarely support the body's weight and can do so only in bursts. With the arms above the head, the heart has to pump up, which means more work for the system. Using the legs, on the other hand, gives the climber greater endurance, something always at a premium on the rock.

When climbing gets hairier, however, the arms and hands become much more important. In certain circumstances, the feet and legs can be used hardly at all. On an overhang, for example, nothing but open space is beneath the rock. Instead, there is a long crack on the rock's underside. You work your way along that, hanging by your hands as if you were on a horizontal ladder, traversing across from rung to rung. If you're lucky and the crack is broad, you can jam your toes in; or possibly there will be some small footholds by which you can keep yourself from swinging. In situations like this, there's no choice: your arms must do most of the work.

As you climb, Dick went on, the more points you have in contact with the wall—ideally, both hands and feet—the more stable you'll be. The *angle* of the body in relation to the rock is also very important. As a rule, your body should be pretty much straight up, because then the force of your weight will be straight down. There is a good reason for this: if the slope of the rock is seventy-five or eighty degrees and your body is also at that angle, the tendency will be for you simply to slide off. But if your body is at ninety degrees, the friction of your feet against the rock (and the stability this creates) will be much greater. On account of this, it is *necessary*, if unnatural, not to hug the rock.

This is even true, actually *more* true, when the pitch is vertical. On a ninety-degree incline, you might have some small hand- and footholds. But you probably wouldn't be able to stand straight up (which would give you no room for maneuvering in any case, as your body would then be flush against the rock). Instead, you would have to lean out on your hands, which is very strenuous. This forces the feet in, so that the rubber of your climbing shoes frictions in against the wall. Even here, especially here, stability actually increases as you push yourself away from the rock (within limits).

These principles sound fine on the ground, of course, but two hundred feet up, on a sheer precipice, our instincts tell us a different story. Naturally, ease in applying these basics comes only with experience. All the same it is by knowing what forces are at work that a climber begins to establish some decision-making capability.

During the day Dick always led and then belayed us as we followed. (Leading is not a prudent idea until you are comfortable on the rock and know how to place the protection properly.) That morning we did one climb on the practice slope and rappelled down — a method of descending a face by means of a rope. Then we did three different, harder climbs right away. It was foggy out. Once we got about fifty feet up on the wall, the carriage road and the ground vanished along with the stark outlines of the bare trees. For our first day of climbing, these conditions were ideal. Because of the fog, we were unable to judge our position relative to the ground, and so the element that causes most beginning climbers the greatest distress — height — was diminished.

Steve and I had done so much reading that much of what we were doing was already familiar. We learned quickly; the height didn't bother us. Climbing was every bit as exciting as my expectation of it. I was ecstatic that day and knew that I had been right. It was what I wanted to do.

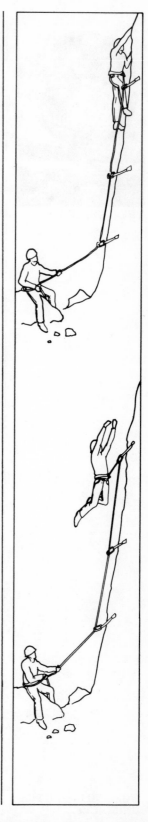

THE UNISPHERE.

Down below, the police seemed to be going about the business of making the best of it, sealing the plaza off, setting up barricades. This relieved me. After all, I didn't want anyone to get hurt; it would have turned adventure into nightmare. As it was, I knew only a thin line divided them. The ease with which the police could close off the plaza below me was actually one reason I'd chosen this particular corner for my climb. There were other reasons: the channels went all the way to the bottom of the building, where I could easily reach them, only at the corners; high wind velocity ruled out the two corners nearest each other (the northwest corner of the south tower and the southeast rim of the northern one); and of the two corners left over the plaza, the northeast corner of the south tower had the better view. (I wanted to be able to see the city, my home in Queens, the countryside all around town).

One hundred and twenty-five feet up now. Randy, Stephen, and Jery were no longer down below, I noticed. Near the corner, several cops, walkie-talkies to their faces, stood looking up at me. This focus of their attention on me made me feel as if I were beneath the center point of a magnifying glass. Five stories above my perch, the sun was shining brightly, still beckoning. This line of the sun, above which no other building cast a shadow, represented a real milestone. When I reached it, I would be well into the climb. It was chilly in the shade. I started climbing again in solitude, in a regular, less frantic way.

The sun caught the aluminum panel on the corner above me and beamed its rays back, reminding me of another structure and another climb.

Nearly two years earlier, I was helping Jery put together a reel of his stunt work in Flushing Meadows Park, site of the 1964 World's Fair (we were filming him performing a number of car gags, as they're called), when, driving by the Unisphere, I happened to look up and notice the way the sunlight shone through its latticework. It occurred to me then that the image would be striking on film, and I started thinking about a picture based on climbing the Unisphere. Jery mentioned it to a film student he knew, who thought it might make an effective commercial for the Environmental Protection Agency. As we planned it, the film would have shown us climbing to the figurative top of the world; then, with a helicopter shot, the camera would pull back to reveal La Guardia Airport (just beyond the Unisphere), with jets taking off, traffic going by, the air dense with smog. "This is a small world," the message would run; "we should take better care of it." Unfortunately, the film maker lost interest and the idea fizzled. It wasn't until months later that Jery happened to mention the idea to Paul Hornstein, another friend, who was a film student at N.Y.U. and looking for a project for a documentary class. Paul became intrigued, and the three of us decided to pool our money and do

WORKING INSIDE THE UNISPHERE.

JERY, SUSPENDED
NEAR AFRICA.

it. This was in the fall of 1976, just after I graduated from St. John's University. Our first step, getting permission from the city, would be the hardest one, we thought.

Climbing all over the Unisphere — 156 feet high, or about the size of a fifteen-story building — didn't sound like the safest of projects, and we were worried that we'd get no further than the Mayor's Office of Film and Television. Bracing ourselves, we made an appointment with Christina Galenti, who was in charge of such things. While her little Pekinese wandered around the office (I petted it sedulously, trying to curry favor),we presented our plan. It was to be a film about two people climbing the Unisphere. Only Jery and I, we promised (falsely), would actually be up on the structure. With the imprimatur of N.Y.U., we would have the protection of a university insurance policy. Ms. Galenti seemed at a loss as to how to respond.

"Are you professional mountain climbers?" she asked.

"Oh, *yeah*," I scoffed. "We have *years* of experience. That's what I do for a living. We know what we're doing. We're no hot dogs."

Ms. Galenti looked at us for a few moments, then decided. "All right," she agreed to our amazement, and gave us permits for two weeks. No authentication of our training or claims was requested. Nothing. It is remarkable, I have discovered, what you can do with official favor under the guise of making a film.

Before she could change her mind we left, practically skipping. We went right to work. Even before the permit took effect, Jery and I brought a forty-foot extension ladder and tools to the Unisphere and I began installing little cable loops around the spot welds on the globe (beneath Antarctica). At this point, I was doing all the aerial work, since Jery's climbing experience was limited. All day long I'd hang happily from the Unisphere, as pedestrians and policemen strolled by. Surprisingly, no one ever questioned what we were doing; perhaps they supposed we were workers.

When filming began, I'd be up on the Unisphere, setting up the shots, by five-thirty or six in the morning. We tried to eliminate from the frame everything that would identify the structure, even the orbits of the globe, to preserve until the last the mystery of our climbing terrain. We used a homemade wooden crane, on which the camera and operator could be raised and lowered, to capture most of the dynamic shots. We bent all the sharp edges on the globe so that they wouldn't hurt the safety ropes we were using.

It was all very time-consuming: putting up shooting platforms inside the Unisphere; teaching a cameraman to climb so that he could reach a shooting position and setting up protection for him; placing ladders from which a person might shoot perpendicular to the orbits; rigging trip mechanisms and safety systems for the falls that Jery and I would do. For wider or more difficult shots, we rented a helicopter and a cherry picker (a mobile crane with a movable platform). In all, the film cost about $5000. During the four weeks of shooting, I spent almost no time on the ground.

The work captivated me. What I found most absorbing was devising ways to get the shots. The substance of the film may have been (no, was) less successful than we'd hoped but from a purely technical point of view, it was enormously satisfying. And the idea has potential, I think. Imagine a car ad, for example. At the end of their ascent, the climbers get into the sedan perched atop the Unisphere (constructed to withstand winds of eighty miles an hour, the structure could easily support an automobile's weight). The camera pulls back. . .

Smack. Slide. Lock.

IN MY HARNESS,
HANGING BELOW
ANTARC

For a couple of weeks after our day with Dick Dumais, Stephen and I talked (and talked) about climbing. At first, we thought we might have Dick take us a few more times, as he'd recommended. Most people train with an experienced climber on a number of climbs until they're comfortable enough to lead and knowledgeable about the procedures and equipment. But then we thought, why bother? Why bother to pay someone for what we felt capable of doing ourselves? Though this might sound foolish, it wasn't. Really, I'd been climbing most of my life. We'd taken to the rock quickly and acquired confidence. I'd studied the mechanics of the equipment in some depth, understood the principles behind it, and, as a practical matter, knew how it all worked. I trusted the strength of the rope. As long as we were careful about putting protection in well and often, I knew we'd be safe.

So we decided to buy our own equipment and simply climb. My days of mooning over gear in climbing shops had taught me what was available. To round out the knowledge, during the past few months I'd gathered a comprehensive collection of climbing equipment catalogues, all carefully indexed and filed. At the Gunks, I'd grilled Dick Dumais about his personal preferences. Still, we took our time now, selecting equipment; our lives would depend on these things and the skill with which we'd use them.

For starters, I selected a 150-foot blue Edelrid nylon rope, made in a kermantle construction (in which an outer sheath surrounds a multitude of inner filaments). These ropes are more expensive than ones made of natural fibers, but they are stronger and thus safer, designed to stretch 80 percent of their length. This type of rope brings a falling climber to a safe, gradual stop, gently breaking his drop. I know one climber who took a 160-foot vertical fall and didn't get hurt a bit. The rope is the single most expensive and important link in the climbing assembly. A good one costs around eighty dollars. It is no place to stint.

After this, I chose a dozen Chouinard nuts in a range of shapes and sizes and selected thin nylon cords in different colors to attach to them—coding chocks in these contrasting colors would help me find what I needed in a hurry. I also selected lengths of one-inch nylon webbing for shoulder slings and for a swami belt. As a scrupulous devotee of the clean-climbing method, I bought no pitons—*I'd* be no spoiler of rock!—but I did purchase a hammer for testing pitons that had been left in the cliffs (as is often the case on established routes). A guidebook to the Schawangunks completed the package, and we were ready.

A few weeks later in the pouring rain, we went climbing on our own for the first time. After studying the guidebook, I'd selected a route called Black Fly. There is a grading system in climbing by which ascents are assigned difficulty factors.

THE SCHAWANGUNKS.

Walking on level ground is called Class 1; Class 2 is rougher ground with a slight slope; Class 3 is steeper, for which you have to use your hands but not a rope; Class 4 is steep but with big holds and ledges (you might want to use a rope, but you don't need to put any protection in the rock). For Class 5 climbing, you use both a rope *and* protection. Formerly, Class 5 climbs were scaled from a low of 5.0 all the way up to 5.10, but as harder climbs were discovered, the scale was extended to 5.12, now considered the ultimate.

Black Fly was a 5.4, much harder than any of the ascents we'd done with Dick Dumais. We knew it would be, but 5.4 meant nothing to us; we wanted to see how difficult it would be, to test how much we were capable of doing.

When I think of that first climb now, I mainly remember the rain and how hard it was coming down. The rock was wet and slippery, and the footholds seemed very small. We didn't even have technical climbing shoes, which are tight-fitting and uncomfortable to walk in but afford intimacy of contact with the rock, increasing the ease and finesse with which you can climb. We wore cumbersome hiking boots.

I led that day. I would put my foot on a small hold and go to make a move, unsure that my foot would really stay there. I was very scared. Then I'd go for the next hold, get it, and exhale, amazed that I was still on the cliff. Certainly I wouldn't be for long, I thought.

All this seemed to require very delicate moves. It seemed extremely precarious and frightening. Now I'd scamper right up Black Fly; I wouldn't even bother to use a rope. The holds would probably look gigantic. But at the time I was right at the edge of my limit. (This sense of terrifying exposure is recaptured with difficulty; climbers push themselves further and further to find it again in new, ever harder climbs.) No kindly fog shielded us now from a stark awareness of the height. The cliff was two hundred feet high and pretty much vertical.

Eighty feet up on the wall, Stephen fell — a short drop of only a foot or two before I caught it. This stuff works! I remember thinking. Suddenly with a fall, theory became real; a climber's confidence in his equipment is never complete until it happens. Aside from the extra drama it gave the ascent, Steve's fall increased my sense of security. More surely now, I felt in control.

All the while as we climbed, it was raining steadily. I recall the rain seeping down the sleeve of my rain parka, running down my arm, soaking my dungarees. It didn't deter us at all. Alone on the rock face, petrified and exhilarated — not an uncommon combination in climbing — we did the whole climb. After coming down from Black Fly, we went to Rock and Snow and, still insatiable, looked at equipment. But in a different way: now we were climbers.

With this under our belts, we couldn't wait to climb in good weather. A couple of weeks later we were back. Our uneasiness at the exposure on Black Fly suggested that we might want to start off with some easier climbs. (A rating of 5.4 meant something to us now.) So we decided to do all the 5.0 climbs at the Gunks and gradually work our way up, improving naturally and systematically. Throughout the spring we went up there just about every other weekend, climbing both Saturdays and Sundays and sleeping in my van parked off the road near the cliffs.

On our early ascents we traded leads, alternating from climb to climb. Often up on the rock, we'd get "gripped"—climbers' lingo for terrified—but this was all to the good; it was what we were after. We wanted to experience that kind of fear, face it, and then move beyond it, accomplishing something important in recognizing that we could.

When you're new to climbing, the height and exposure can be overwhelming, and just getting up the cliff seems hard enough. Still, there is an aesthetic in the sport; even as a beginner, Dick Dumais had told us, you must attempt to get up with some style. Form is very important. So we tried not to use our knees when we got to a ledge but to climb with our feet as he'd instructed us; to use only the rock—avoiding the temptation of clinging to trees—and to make the climb as pure as we possibly could.

We began to learn how to look at the rock and how to read it, so that we could use it to our advantage. With a little experience, options start to open up; holds appear where none were visible. After a while, what once appeared to be a slick unapproachable surface becomes a road map.

Although we hadn't nearly exhausted the 5.0 climbs at the Gunks, we were soon sprinkling in 5.1 and 5.2 climbs. Then, after we'd been climbing three or four weekends, we did a 5.5 climb—with an overhang—called Shockley's Ceiling (first scaled by William S., whose theories on the intelligence of blacks, which he proposed was genetically inferior to that of whites, has brought him a more complicated celebrity than his ascent).

Why shouldn't we have tried it? The worst that might have happened was that one or both of us would take a fall. Climbers have an expression, "C'mon, let's go fall off something," for trying something hard. If you don't attempt these things, you'll never improve or find out what you can do. Perhaps because I was innately so comfortable on the rock, perhaps because I was lucky, I didn't take a fall of any kind for several months. This is of no importance. If you're really testing yourself, eventually you'll fall and learn something from it.

Ordinarily, you become most frightened in climbing when it isn't possible to put in protection for a long distance (if it is possible, there is really little to be afraid of). Perhaps your last piece of protection is twenty or thirty feet below you, and it is necessary to do a "thin" move, in which the holds are small; you are hanging only by your fingertips, which is very strenuous, and you have one or two moves ahead of you until you can reach a "bucket," a big hand- or foothold. It is then that you begin to anticipate falling and the doubts creep in. *This is really thin, too thin*, you say to yourself. *Am I strong enough? I'm not strong enough! I hope I don't get too tired before I reach the bucket. I don't think I can make it. I'm tiring too fast! I don't see how I can do it.*

But then you do it anyway, you reach the belay ledge, and the excitement and satisfaction come flooding in. You think, *Whoooooh!* I almost didn't make it. I almost took a *screamer!* But, of course, you did make it. You managed to push beyond your fear, and there is no feeling like it.

Being afraid is a natural, self-protective reaction, and while climbing I'm often afraid. But fear doesn't always have to be negative. It feels good to have the adrenaline running while climbing. It feels good to get past that fear. It feels good to have the air beneath your feet.

RAPPELLING OFF ANATHEMA IN YO-SEMITE VALLEY.

It was pretty quiet now. The first wave of commotion had subsided, and only occasional sounds filtered up to me from the street. It seemed very strange up there. I was completely, *completely* alone, more alone than I had felt in my life. Just now, I was in a curious middle zone, an untouchable waiting ground. At the bottom before I had raced above the one-hundred-foot mark, I had averted being seized, but what I was hurrying toward was certain capture at the other end. In between, however, I was my own man, more so than I'd ever been. Like anything else, liberty seems most intense when you know its exact end. And now, for a short while, every restraint, every tie, seemed to have been shrugged off, suspended. It was a 1350-foot strip of total freedom.

Two more steps, one more ... up, and I was in the warm sun. Leaning back from the devices, I slipped my pack off, opened the top pocket, and took out a quart bottle of water. My mouth was getting very dry, but I had to ration myself; I wanted some water left for the later part of the climb. After a few sips, I put the bottle back in the pack. In there with it were two health-food candy bars already two years old; but I wasn't hungry. I slipped my pack on and resumed climbing.

The crowds were starting to gather now behind the police lines as people began going to work. The streets were filling up quickly.

Push. Slide. Step up.

Even now, I was having a hard time believing I was doing this. As I climbed, I'd look up, down, hang back, and feel myself on the wall of the tower. For so many months as I'd been planning it, the climb had seemed a phantom, too unrealistic and ambitious to expect to really happen. Now I was laughing to myself, cackling out loud, for here I was. I was happy that I'd be the first to do it. So many things, it had seemed, might go wrong and prevent me from doing it. Whenever I looked at the silver corner of the tower, I'd try to imagine what it would be like up there. In situations like this one, you build up an image, projecting forward, that is so intense it can be hard to fill; reality can seem a little pale beside it. Credulity sometimes hangs back stubbornly.

In this case, the work made the climb real. The blisters forming on my hands were no memory or dream. The climb was a *lot* of work. And I didn't seem to be getting anywhere. Ventilation sections divide each World Trade Center tower into thirds; it is as if three buildings, 450 feet each, are stacked on top of each other. I was still a long way from the first divider. Boy, I'm tiring, I thought, and I'm not even one third of the way up. I kept checking my progress in relation to the other tall buildings around the Center. My progress seemed very slow. I began to worry about whether I would make it; from my present perch, some twenty stories above the ground, the tower looked overwhelming. Its corner, seen from my vantage point, tapers sharply to a point; the journey looked endless. Sisyphus came to mind. It seemed possible to me then that I'd be here forever, climbing up, sliding down, climbing up again.

I decided not to think too much about my progress or my doubts. With mental discipline you can do almost anything. I knew that. I'd done many other harder climbs. Out in Yosemite there is a climb called Lunatic Fringe (a 5.10), which I thought of now. It is a short climb, only two hundred feet or so. Its salient feature is a thin finger crack, the fissure in the rock by which you ascend. From the bottom, the crack looks no more substantial than a long hair; on either side, the rock is smooth with no holds at all. It could hardly appear more intimidating. Right from the start of the climb I thought, I'm gonna fail on this one.

But I kept going. I kept thinking, I'll probably fall any second. My arms were "pumped up"—an expression climbers use to describe exhaustion—and my fingers were hardly working. It was a straight-up wall. I'd get myself in a stance, with my fingers in the crack system and my feet on small holds. Then I'd remove one hand, shake it out to rest it a little, put it back in the crack, and take the other one out, by which time the first hand would be tired again. *You've got to go for it*, I'd think. *Go a little higher*. As I did, I was putting in plenty of protection. All the while I was terrified of not making it, a fear that grew larger all the time. Because the closer you get to a goal, the more heartbreaking it seems if you don't make it. Sometimes that alone keeps you pushing. *I don't want to give up*, I'd think. *There is something about this climb. If I give up, it's gonna destroy me.* At this moment, my whole attitude on life seemed to depend on making that climb. I was frenzied, hyperventilating, going crazy with exertion. And when I got to the ledge, the end of the climb, I collapsed. It was failing that had been scaring me, not falling; failing to complete something into which I had poured so much energy. Something that I wanted to do so much. Something like this.

Smack. Push. Step. This one is only a matter of stamina, I thought. The only new elements here were the distractions, which would soon grow greater, the possibility of interference, and the novelty of the wall. I put my doubts away and became absorbed in the process of the climb.

While I was learning to climb, I was working as a model maker for Ark Research. I'd come to this job circuitously, through the same combination of good luck and happenstance that had led me to so many of the things I've done. Certainly I never thought I'd work in medical research. I never set out to be a toy designer. I never focused my energies toward one career. Curiously, what I would do never worried me. Chance always seemed to lead me along engaging paths, to pursuits that tapped my strengths and interests.

In college at State University at Farmingdale (a Long Island junior college that my father had attended), I studied ornamental horticulture (those visions of the tropics still held me). At the time, the natural thing would have been for me to attend St. John's, a Catholic university where my mother worked as a secretary and the tuition would have been free. But horticulture, which St. John's didn't offer, was all I wanted to study, and Farmingdale was the only place I wanted to do it. When I was a kid my father and I used to go out there to visit the greenhouse, filled with tropical trees and plants, and the college farm, where he'd studied agriculture. Eventually, perhaps, I'd be a botanist, I thought, doing plant research in the jungles of South America. Or I'd raise tropical plants in greenhouses. At any rate, I decided to spend the money I'd saved from working summers as an air-conditioner installer on college and, at Farmingdale, for the first time I did quite well as a student. A simple equation here: because I was paying for it, it meant more to me. For the first time, really, I was doing things out of choice, directing my own life. It was an important decision.

When I graduated, two years later in 1969, instead of doing plant research in the jungle, I worked as a laborer in a greenhouse. Even for a summer job it was terrible, lugging things around for minimum wage. My morning arrival became erratic. I started growing a beard. My hair was long. My boss, an exceptionally straitlaced German, grew displeased with my attitude and advancing shagginess. The final straw came in late summer when I made an extended visit to the Woodstock music festival. Time slipped away there. How important was a miserable job in the face of an *event*? Moving in a caravan that inched north, it had taken my friends and I eight hours to drive up there (ordinarily, it was a two-and-a-half-hour trip); we took the car as far as we could, then abandoned it and walked a couple of miles. Everywhere people were getting stoned (among other things). The rain came down steadily, but I took the canvas roof from a deserted concession stand, made a tent, and we stayed dry. All day and night, the loud, loud music played around us. As we went to sleep, Paul Butterfield might be playing; when we awoke it would be Jimi Hendrix. Performers, even those who hadn't been scheduled to appear, arrived one after the other, drawn by the rapidly

WITH MY MOTHER, IN LINA WERTMULLER GLASSES, AT MY GRADUATION FROM FARMINGDALE.

50

WOODSTOCK

circulating news of the remarkable thing that was taking place. I'd never been particularly into the whole peace movement, never been political, never felt much connection with any of the things for which that period and this festival are now celebrated, but it was impossible not to be taken up by it. Here, you felt, a peace sign *meant* something. I didn't smoke dope, didn't drink. Nothing. It made no difference. People were open with each other, friendly in a way I'd never known, and on a scale, of course, that no one would encounter again. There was an exhilarating sense of belonging. It was clear that something exceptional was taking place.

When I returned to my job a day late, I was fired. (Obviously my boss hadn't been mellowing out at Woodstock.) No matter; the summer was almost over anyway. In the early fall I enrolled at St. John's with the idea of getting a B.A. in psychology. My thinking here—exactly where the imagined appeal of psychology lay—escapes me now, but in any case, after a few months I dropped out. St. John's had the same kind of desk as the parochial grammar school I'd gone to, and I felt as if I was back *there*. I just wasn't ready for it then; I didn't want to be in school

Now I had to find work again. Soon I was offered two jobs, equally enthralling; one was at a carpet warehouse, another at a plastic-bag factory. Unable to decide, I accepted both, then finally settled on the bag factory while driving to work on the morning I was to report. I soon grew bored with this and got a job with a plant shop in the city, taking care of plants in offices around town. It paid terribly, I hated commuting to Manhattan, and I began going in later and later each day (does this pattern sound familiar?) until finally one morning I was so late for work that the office called. Where was I? It had come to a head, but somehow I couldn't tell the truth, that I disliked the work, hated coming into the city for so little pay, that it just was too draining. These facts were too bald; I had to make something up.

So I told them I had narcolepsy. Where this came from, I don't know. I'd once read a little squib about it and now, for some reason, I remembered it. What's *narcolepsy*? they asked. In some detail, I recounted the sad story of my sleeping sickness. The amphetamines had worked for a while, I told them. But now they seemed to have lost their effectiveness. There was little I could do. "I don't know if you'll want me any more," I said, "as I have this trouble waking up." I felt *terrible* doing this. I'm really not a compulsive liar, yet I felt I had to get out of it gracefully.

I don't know if my boss believed me or not. "Oh," she said, "well, uh, yeah. I guess we can't hold onto you with something like that."

So I was free again, out of work, still living with my parents. I started looking for another job. Then I saw a little ad: "Trainee for making prototypes." Since I enjoyed building things, I figured I'd give it a shot.

People always told me to dress up for interviews, to make an effort to appear presentable, but I went to Ark Research in dungarees and a t-shirt. I met the foreman and we wound up talking about model railroads, which fascinated him, and building racing cars. I had a dreadful work record, as the preceding should have indicated. I'd worked in a lot of places for only a short time, and my recommendations could be charitably characterized as poor. But Bob and I hit if off, and he hired me anyway. I stayed there for six years.

Ark was a new division of an old company—102 years old when I joined it—but this latest department was not to be what kept it in business. Not that we weren't productive. During my time there, we turned out all kinds of items (for which I and a few others would build the prototypes): vacuum devices with bubbling chambers; heart valves; colostomy bags; ingenious syringes (on which the plungers would have to be completely depressed before they could be pulled out, insuring a full injection); little hooks and stands for the ends of hospital beds; batteries and pumps for a portable breathing apparatus for people who'd gotten wounded in the field.

The thing was, though, that very few of these devices ever hit the market. We'd make reports, we'd design things, produce them, waste time and money testing them, go through all the motions, but it was all a fantasy. We were just a toy shop for the president of the company, an indulgence, an idea that pleased him. And so there was an unreal quality to what we were doing; we played around, had long lunches, held entertaining brain-storming sessions, eventually came up with solutions to interesting problems, and built our inventions. But they went no farther than our shop. Still, for a long while the work suited me. Confronting mechanical and technical problems, constructing things, was what I'd been doing most of my life for fun. The only difference was that now I was doing it for a living.

SHAGGY, AT ARK RE-
SEARCH.

"**G**o, *George. Go!*" Twenty-five stories up now, I knew that voice. Unmistakably, it belonged to Ron Di Giovanni, my balloonist friend. Apparently, he had arrived there late. I smiled to myself. Ron is nervous, excitable, prone to quick enthusiasm, and now his personality bounded out.

We'd met the previous summer in an unusual way. I'd been idly scanning the help-wanted section of the *Long Island Press* one morning searching for the job of my dreams, when my eyes stopped short. Here it was: "Hot Air Balloonist Looking for Crew." Incredulous, I stared at the ad. I called right away. Ron, who hoped to become a professional balloonist doing promotional work—something like flying the Lark balloon—told me he needed an assistant, someone to help him get started and follow the balloon once it was airborne. We set a date to meet in the parking lot from which, weather permitting, he planned to take off. Along with a friend of his, and Randy, who had come along with me, I helped him inflate the balloon.

Ron is a good spirit and loyal friend, entirely well meaning, but he could never be described as calm. As he cracked orders, I scurried around doing whatever he instructed, pleased to be connected to something like this at all. On that morning it was too foggy to fly, and we had to pack up the balloon. Ron liked the way I threw myself into things, however, and we set another date about a week later.

Early on the second morning, when it was still quite dark out—ideally, a balloon is inflated early, when the air is still calm—we loaded the balloon, gondola, and other flying paraphernalia into and on my station wagon and drove out to Mitchell Field at Nassau Community College. Once again, Ron imperiously snapped out orders—it didn't take long to learn that this would be the norm—and I raced around, hopping to his bidding. We inflated the balloon. On this occasion I was to go up in the balloon with him, as I did on many later flights. It was a time of high excitement for me. I'd never been in anything smaller than a commercial jet before, much less a craft as beguiling as a hot-air balloon.

"Now relax," Ron said nervously as we took off. I was totally relaxed. "Don't let the height bother you," he advised as we climbed higher and the view opened up pleasantly. Once we were safely on our way, Ron let me take control—a word too strong to describe what happens in a balloon, a wonderfully whimsical form of transport that floats where the winds will have it go—with the burner. As the air cools inside the balloon, the balloon begins to drop; when the air is heated, the balloon rises. It is important to heat the air at just the right time. Good fliers can keep the path of the balloon—its altitude—fairly steady. In the hands of novices, the balloon generally rises and falls. Although a climb meter and altimeter are part of a gondola's standard equipment, it's usually easier to gauge what you're doing by watching the horizon and the trees. We

ordinarily flew at three hundred feet; it was nice to stay low and enjoy the view.

As the morning wore on and the sun came up and out, we flew over Salisbury Park, east of our takeoff point, and over the various highways that ribbon the island. Car horns would beep, and people would wave as we passed. Between blasts of the burner, it was very still; then that deafening roar would come and a moment later, it would be quiet again.

After about a half hour, Ron started looking for a place to land. Anxiously (for a change) he was watching the fuel tanks; a balloon's burner consumes propane at a great rate, and the supply does not last long. As Ron scanned the area around us, I manned the burner. "Give it some heat!" he'd shriek at me, and I'd give it a blast. A balloon accelerates as it falls, so it's necessary to offset that momentum. Since it takes about twelve seconds for the heat to rise up, warm the air inside the balloon, and affect the craft's trajectory, it's necessary to fly well ahead of oneself. A moment after the first order, Ron would snap another: "Give it some more!" Each time the balloon would veer up sharply. Now it took on a path resembling a Mig's evasive maneuvers. We'd give it too much heat then open the vent to compensate and the craft would drop down too much as it cooled off. However eccentric our course, it was very peaceful floating along and seemed absolutely safe to me. All the time however, Ron kept telling me to relax; he seemed to have entered entirely into the anxiety he expected to discover in me. My only concern was that he might pop something under the pressure.

"Do you know the island?" he asked.

"Pretty well," I said. Ron had a road map, but this part of the island was as familiar to me as my front yard.

"Do you know a place where we could land?"

"There's a park up there." I pointed.

Ron shook his head, remonstrating. "You *never* know where you're going to land until you get there."

"Okay" I laughed. "Then the heck with it."

Now we were drifting over backyards—sometimes as low as one hundred feet—with no landing place in sight, and Ron's nervousness began to grow. It was still early. Women oblivious of our passage were hanging clothes out to dry as we floated by above them. Then the blast of our burn would sound—it probably seemed as if a Phantom jet were passing just above their heads—and they'd look up in alarm. Cars started following us, dogs barked, kids took up the chase on bicycles and foot, and soon a few police cars were trailing us as well. Anything that was such conspicuous fun had to be breaking *some* law. At last, the parking lot of a Sears Roebuck came into view. On our approach, we shaved it a bit tight, scraping along the top limbs of a large tree. "Hold on! Hold on!" Ron screamed. "Take it easy! Hold on really tight!" Then we started to come down steeply. "Bend your knees now, bend your knees! Hold on!

Take it easy! It's gonna be okay!" The gondola hit hard as we landed in the parking lot, and I stepped out. People gathered around and helped us pack up the balloon. In a moment, the police arrived, then representatives of the FAA, whom the police had summoned. In vain: search as they might, we'd broken no laws.

Each time after this that Ron went flying I would take him to the location, fill up the propane tanks, do whatever needed to be done, then usually assist him on the flight. For which he paid me ten dollars. I couldn't believe anyone would pay me, even nominally, for something that was such pure pleasure. On every flight, police helicopters would soon be inspecting us and police cars would greet us, and the same round of explanations and questions would ensue. Officials remained unconvinced that drifting around this way in a colorful idiosyncratic craft, landing wherever the wind took you, could be legal. Crowds always followed us when we flew, responding to the sight of a balloon with childlike delight. From time to time, especially when our landing place was particularly unusual, we'd be in the papers.

Ron's most notorious excursion took place in late December of that same year, 1976, when I was working at Ideal Toy. A few days before the event, Ron telephoned me to ask if I'd assist him with a flight he was planning—over Manhattan. Would I help him get launched? Of course, I told him, pleased at the prospect of another adventure. On the morning he'chosen, December 23, I rose at five and picked him up with all his equipment; we crossed the Verrazano-Narrows Bridge from Brooklyn to Staten Island in search of a place from which he might set off. Soon we found a good spot, not far from the northern coast, and inflated.

Moments later, with four full tanks of propane, Ron took off. As he started over Staten Island, staying low, I followed him in my car. The direction of the wind was perfect, taking him right toward Manhattan. He was drawing a bead directly on his desired course. It was a nice sunny day, exceptionally warm for this time of year. (It's often warmer up in a balloon than on the ground; since you travel with the wind you feel it less forcefully—it seems still.) The breeze was light, yet strong enough to keep the balloon moving. From the edge of Staten Island, I watched Ron fly over the harbor toward Manhattan, still on course.

Rushing to a phone booth then, I called *The New York Times*, the *Daily News*, the *New York Post*, and several radio and television stations. Though Ron hadn't asked me to do this, I knew he would want it; if he was going to get into advertising, what better way than through a little self-promotion? "There's a balloon going right toward Manhattan!" I told them. "A hot-air balloon, and it's over New York Harbor."

Their interest was immediate. "Can we see it from Manhattan?" they asked.

RON'S BALLOON DRIFTING ACROSS NEW YORK HARBOR TOWARD MANHATTAN.

"Probably from Battery Park," I told them.

"Who's flying it?"

I told them. Some of them asked my name as well. "Why is he doing it?" everyone questioned.

"To have a good time," I said. Which was true.

Soon a number of reporters were down at the Battery. Some stations sent out helicopters with film crews and photographers. Ron headed northwest, past the Battery and up the Hudson River. Then the wind shifted, drawing him over toward the World Trade Center towers, and he had to raise the balloon. ("Give it a blast!" I could imagine him snapping at himself.) As helicopters followed, he went up over the two buildings. The police were outraged and helpless, which probably accounted for their fury in the first place. Ron crossed over the spires of lower Manhattan and drifted up the East River. His initial intention had been to go all the way to Connecticut, flying very low beneath the air lanes, but the wind had another plan and he landed near a Con Ed plant in Long Island City, on the east bank of the East River across from midtown. That evening Ron's story was on local television stations; the next morning, he appeared in the centerfold of the *Daily News* and in newspapers around the country. As a result of this exploit, in which he'd violated air traffic rules, his balloonist's license was suspended.

The morning of the flight, I arrived late to work. People there had been listening to the radio and knew all about what I'd been up to. As I entered, they smiled indulgently. What could you expect from someone who spent his weekends hanging from precipices!

Now, in a gesture so natural for him, Ron was here to cheer *me* on. "*The police are putting. . .*" I thought I heard him call, then no more. After a moment, I started climbing again.

Ron's rooting was more costly than mine had been. The police arrested him.

Our minds are devious in inventing reasons for us not to do things, convincing us that we should not even try. It happens to me when I climb. I think, Why am I *doing* this? Why am I putting myself in this position? The "wall" that runners speak of—the physical limit, about nineteen miles, beyond which the body is supposedly incapable of running is an example of this. Many experienced marathoners now say the wall is a myth. Yet runners talk about it so much that when they're racing they become afraid of it; and, anticipating it, they begin to create it. They start to tire, gradually persuading themselves they cannot go on. Why can't they?

Experienced runners say that rather than ignoring fatigue, the best thing to do is to stay attuned to it, be aware of what's happening—how your legs feel, how your breathing is coming. Focus on the process, not the limitation, they say, and you'll avoid the treacherous impasse of the wall. Certainly, the regularity with which thousands complete marathons each year, not to mention races of over a hundred miles, ought to satisfy us that the only walls are within our minds and of our own making.

Shockley's Ceiling was a case in point for Steve and me, the kind of example that climbing provides all the time. We were a hair away from failure on it, yet made it. And another wall faded away.

ON THE WEST BUT-
TRESS OF THE BAS-
TILLE, ELDORADO
SPRINGS CANYON,
COLORADO.

The crowd was growing all the time as nine o'clock approached. Hundreds, perhaps thousands—it was hard to tell—were gathered down below. On the plaza, the police had inflated an air bag, about twenty-five feet square. From my point of view, around 250 feet up, it looked like a pincushion. This precaution amused me; the wind was blowing twenty or thirty miles an hour now, forcibly enough to blow me a good distance. Even without the wind, the chances of my landing on the bag in a fall were minuscule (only slightly greater, perhaps, than the bag's effectiveness from this height should I by some accident happen to find my way to it).

But what else could the police do? Because they had the air bag, they inflated it; to me, it was an indication of their helplessness. I was sympathetic. I was causing a great deal of agitation, I could see, complicating a great many lives. I felt rather bad about it, but I couldn't stop now: it was something I had to do.

Since we'd been able to do Shockley's Ceiling, a 5.5, now Steve and I decided to try a 5.6. We chose High Exposure, a climb that Dick Dumais had described as a real classic, one of his favorites. If it became too difficult, we figured we could always rappel down.

The Schawangunks guidebook features photographs of the rock, with lines indicating the ascent routes superimposed on the pictures. Even so, it isn't hard to get confused, as we found when we mistakenly took a route that went off to the right, a *5.9* ascent called Directissima (5.9, you'll remember, is just a shade less demanding than what used to be considered the ultimate in rock climbing). At this point, we had only been climbing for five or six weekends. Certainly it *looked* scary, but the appearance of a climb is deceptive. Often a route will look easy but then as you begin climbing you find that what from the bottom seemed to be good handholds are actually "upside-down holds," or cracks into which you can't put your fingers. On the rock, your perspective changes.

So we set out. The climb was just one point above Shockley's, I reasoned (falsely). How much harder could it be? (Much.) Directissima was very steep with a horizontal crack (beneath an overhang) by which you traversed around a corner. The rock was smooth with only the crack for holds; this made for strenuous climbing. As I edged up, I tried to friction my feet against the face, but they weren't holding well. In a situation like this one, when you're hanging by your fingertips, your forearms become exhausted quickly ("blown," as climbers say); you become convinced your strength won't last, you're not going to make it. Which is exactly what I was thinking as I came around the corner.

I was *terrified*. So much so that, lacking good holds, I grabbed onto pitons that had been left in the rock. This may not sound like a big deal (it may, in fact, sound like common sense), but among climbers it's considered highly unethical. This was what is called a "free" climb. The protection and rope were only there as a back-up, a safety system to catch me in a fall but not to help me climb. I wasn't using the pitons to pull myself up, as I would in an "aid" or "artificial" climb, as it's also known. Aid climbing is considered less pure, more technological. It establishes barriers between you and the rock. It places the emphasis on the equipment, rather than a climber's resourcefulness. It lacks poetry. At the Gunks, once an artificial climb has been done without aid, no one wants to touch it in any other way. It would seem like taking an ocean liner on a sailboat race.

On a free climb, my grabbing those pitons was cheating. At the time, I did it gratefully. At least, I told myself, I hadn't pounded them into the rock.

Hanging now on the face of the cliff, I was breathing heavily, looking ahead, and thinking: If only I could get up there to that little ledge, I could probably stand up and rest a little and think about it. I could have backed down, of course. The climb was hard enough so that there would have been no shame in it (nor is there ever, really; when a climber's psychological attitude and physical stamina seem inadequate, retreating is only good judgment). But I couldn't bear to now. I wanted to succeed.

At this point I didn't have a ledge to stand on; I was simply hanging, fifty feet up or so, with only an occasional foothold and the thin crack to grasp onto. At length, I reached a belay ledge.

"This is *hard*," I called down to Stephen. "If this is 5.6 I don't know when we're going to be able to do it regularly." But I thought perhaps the hardest part of the climb, the 5.6 portion, was over.

I had my doubts. When Steve got up to the ledge, he saw what I'd been looking at; a big wall, directly ahead. There were holds, but it was terribly steep, actually beyond the vertical with a slight overhang, which meant we'd have to use our arms most of the time. We stood staring at it for a while; it didn't look *impossible*. The next ledge was visible, as were the big holds by which we could reach it, and along the way there were fixed pitons so that we could clip in quickly for protection. Even if we fell, the protection looked reassuringly good.

I figured I'd attempt it. In a situation like this, I'm almost always willing to go for it. If it's too difficult for me, I'd prefer to fall than to give up.

Steve set up a belay position, and I started climbing. I was really scared now, looking straight down and hanging by my fingers. When I clipped my rope into the last piton, about ten feet from the final ledge, I let myself hang there for a while by a sling; I had little strength left. Steve watched worriedly, as he belayed me. Perhaps he was thinking of the climb ahead of him, too. Finally I collected myself, made a final push and reached the ledge, where I collapsed in exhaustion.

This ledge was a triangular point of rock that stuck out like a ship's prow, one side of which—the side I'd just come up—was overhanging. After catching my breath, I tied in and stood on the corner and looked down at Steve seventy feet below.

Steve began climbing as I belayed. I don't know whether his strength went or he got psyched out, but when he was at the last piece of protection—the one that I had paused to hold onto—he fell. When he dropped, he swung way out, all the way around the prow, forty feet or so. Although I was holding him, I didn't have the belay set tightly enough; had I lost my footing, his fall would have pulled me down on my knees, almost certainly injuring me. (This incident taught me a good deal about belaying; what I *should* have done was tied myself in a lot tighter to the anchor. This way, Steve's weight would have been transferred to the anchor not to my legs.)

As I held him, Steve swung back and forth in large arcs out in open space. My legs were straining now. "Get back to the rock as soon as you can," I called to him. He gradually worked his way back to the face, and I lowered him to the ledge and rappelled down to him; then we rappelled down off the climb together.

If that was a 5.6, we agreed, we had a lot of work ahead before we'd be doing that kind of thing comfortably. (Weeks later, when we discovered our mistake, I was ebullient; with just a bit of cheating I'd gotten up there. A 5.9!) Had I known this at the start, I would never have been able to do it. Those tricks of the mind again.

That night, I had a nightmare about Steve's fall. Only then was I scared, when the excitement was gone, the adrenaline no longer pumping, and I could regard the fall in its plainer aspects. What was frightening, of course, was the clear potential for disaster. Had the belay not been set up correctly, Steve's fall could easily have pulled me off the ledge, and we would both have been killed.

This fear after we were safely down accorded with my regular anxiety pattern. Lying in bed, remembering the climbs of the weekend just past, I'd think, "This is crazy. I don't know if I want to do this any more." But the next morning, those doubts would be gone. All week long, I'd look forward to the weekend, when I'd be climbing again.

For now I was going up to the Gunks every week. Often alone, as Steve wasn't fanatical about it the way I was. He had a girl friend; he had other interests in life; there were other people he wanted to be spending time with. I was seeing a girl then too, but everything in my life took a backseat to climbing. Nothing could compare with it for me.

ROSY CRUCIFIXION, A 5.10 CLIMB AT EL-DORADO SPRINGS CANYON. I'M ASCEN-DING BY MEANS OF A VERTICAL CRACK.

My concern now, besides bulling my way up the building, was that the police might attempt to come down and reach me from the top. There is a scaffolding, larger than the automatic window washer and designed to envelop it, that maintenance people use to service the washer when it malfunctions. This scaffolding was what I thought the police might lower. The prospect didn't cause me great apprehension. One of the reasons I'd selected a corner to climb was that I knew the scaffolding wouldn't fit there; the apparatus was too wide. Still, I wasn't certain that there wasn't something else that might fit. And so as I climbed I also watched, wary of what the police might do.

Push. A third of the way up now, I was very elated. Every so often I'd stop and try to hold onto the moment, freeze it. At last I was high on the tower, and all around the view had opened up. To the north, beyond the low warehouses, old factories, and tenements sprinkled around the lower west side, were Soho and Greenwich Village, with the green of Washington Square and the Arch, which seemed tiny now, at its northern rim. Beyond it, Fifth Avenue cut a swath obliquely away toward the Empire State Building, and to the northeast, the beautiful Art Deco silver spire of the Chrysler Building glistened in the sun: between 1931 and 1933 the tallest building in the world, it was now dwarfed by structures everywhere around. The Atlantic had begun to be visible beyond Brooklyn and Queens, and Long Island stretched off to the east. Across the Hudson to the west were the Jersey plains, and, just north of the dramatic Palisades, the Hudson Highlands began to roll. The day had the clarity of cut glass. At times, taking all this in I felt beside myself.

To my surprise, as I climbed I occasionally noticed numerals on the stainless-steel panels. These notations were erratic, so at first I wasn't sure what they indicated; but by the time I was one quarter of the way up I was certain they were floor numbers. Someone had penciled them in, perhaps as a guide to the construction workers installing the panels. This human touch was unexpected here. It was like coming across a bottle with a message on a deserted beach. An indirect yet affecting contact with someone who would always be unknown.

I had settled into the cadence of the climb. From time to time, I looked down at the dense crowds, the cars, and the congestion all around the open plaza. How much of this was due to me and how much to the normal rush-hour press, I couldn't tell. Certainly the crowds were large, filling the streets all around the building. Traffic was going by very slowly. People were stopping to watch, getting out of their cars and trucks, beeping their horns. I didn't wave back, not yet. At this point it would have seemed gratuitous, self-glorification, like calling, "Hey, look at me!" I felt good enough as it was.

Rest came easily. Every so often, I'd just lean back, relax, and take a sip of water. I was wearing old rock-climbing shoes, good ones— Royal Robbins Yosemite shoes made by Galibier in France; the first pair of climbing shoes, in fact, that I ever owned—with stiff soles that made them suitable for what I was doing, standing in stirrups and slings. However, the stirrups were drawn around my feet with necessarily tight slip knots, and my feet were beginning to blister where they were bound. As best I could, I kept moving my feet around in them. Once in a while, I'd stop to readjust the stirrups and change where the weight was being loaded.

The noises of the street were gradually fading as I ascended, and the low hum of air-conditioning units atop adjacent buildings was replacing them. That sound apart, it was very quiet. The higher I climbed, the stronger the breezes were, but the sun was warm on my face and I was comfortable as long as I kept moving.

Punch. Slide. Pushing a device higher in the channel, I looked up and saw it: the scaffolding was being brought around the side of the building. (A dolly running along tracks shuttles it around the lip of the building's roof.) The scaffolding began on the east wall to my left, came around the corner directly over me, and settled on the north wall just to my right. It was possible to see it hanging over the edge. Perhaps seventy stories above me, it was a tiny speck; I couldn't tell if it was growing larger (which would mean, of course, that they had begun to lower it).

Ah well, I had a plan for such a contingency, a diversionary move that would place me beyond the reach of the police. Now I was feeling like an outlaw for sure. I felt in control though. It wasn't an unpleasurable sensation. Not at all.

Very soon after I started climbing, I realized that it was giving my life new meaning. It altered my attitude about myself and the world around me. I took increased charge of my life because I was taking charge of it every weekend on the high walls, relying on myself in situations of the greatest immediacy. This gave me a sense of self-confidence, a new feeling of accomplishment and purpose that filtered down into other things. It made me feel better about myself. For the first time, I had a focus.

People can find this challenge, this target for their abilities in any number of things, of course. But climbing combined what I'd always liked anyway: the outdoors, technical problem-solving that required ingenuity, dealing with mechanics through the equipment, doing something rigorous, confronting fear. It taxed me in ways I found most satisfying. It always posed new and harder problems.

Moreover, climbing is a sport without being a game. It is not a competitive situation; the only opponents are your own self-doubts. "After World War II Americans gave their enthusiasm to group sports," Pete Hamill has observed, writing about boxing. "Baseball went continental, with teams spreading to the west coast, the southwest and Canada. Football became the most popular sport of the 50's and 60's. And its group violence paralleled the violent expansionism of the United States around the world. . . . With the sudden growth of group sports and the submersion of the individual by the group impulse, boxing waned."

Climbing cuts right across the grain of this trend, which is just what I like about it. It is in no sense contrived: there is no artifice. There are no invented rules and obstacles and terms of victory. It's a very free, unstructured sport. There are only the rock and a distance to be traveled, and the challenge is in the difficulty of the ascent. No clock runs. There are no points. No fouls. No opponents to beat. No one wins at another's expense. The only competition is with yourself, what's going on in your own mind. It is a question, finally, of a person's will and of the tenacity and resourcefulness with which he asserts it.

STEPHEN WILLIG AND STEVE MATOUS WORKING ON A BOULDERING PROBLEM.

Calmly, I took my pack off and clipped it into one of my devices. I took out a rope. Moving slowly and methodically—I was being very careful not to drop anything—I unclipped myself from one of the devices, and, using a figure-eight knot and a carabiner, attached the rope to it. Next, I took out a pair of Gibbs Ascenders—devices that lock onto a line (compressing it in much the same way as my climbing instruments pressed the steel of the channels)—and secured them to the rope. One at a time, I transferred the slings and stirrups from my devices to the Gibbs Ascenders. Then I detached myself from the other device in the channel. At this point, I was hanging off the rope by the Gibbs Ascenders.

Since both my harness and my feet (in the stirrups) were attached to the ascenders, it took no effort to maintain my position. I could simply hang there as before with my hands free.

I uncoiled about thirty feet of rope and hung the rest over the devices. Then I worked my way down fifteen or twenty feet, using the ascenders. This required no great adjustment in technique; the Gibbs Ascenders worked the same way as my devices. As I lowered myself slowly, the crowd did not noticeably react. Had I rappelled down, taking the distance quickly in a few big leaps, playing hopscotch on the wall, it might have stirred things up a little.

My next move would be to swing over on the rope to the other side of the building, right to left. Anticipation of the maneuver scared me. Now another mechanism had become involved in the climb, and some of the simplicity of my methods had been lost; naturally, the more equipment you use, the greater the possibility for error. The move I had planned was familiar in *type* to me from climbing. But it was definitely a new wrinkle in the ascent, and there could be no mistakes, no second-guessing.

Originally when I was preparing for the climb, I thought that if circumstances required I swing over on the rope—a pendulum—to elude the police, I would lower myself on 150 feet of rope and take a gigantic, spectacular swing on it;—the World Trade Center would become my play-gym; if I was going to become an outlaw, my crime would be one of dramatic gestures. But I decided I didn't want to freak out the crowd, and I didn't want to freak out myself either. What's more, the move would have been tiring. Afterward, I would have had to climb up that 150 feet again. My palms and legs told me no. For this morning, 110 stories seemed like enough.

Taking a gentle swing, really walking my way across the surface of one panel, I worked myself around to the left-hand side of the corner and over to the building's east face. On either side of the windows there and everywhere on the wall of the tower, aluminum flutings extend out about a foot. Holding onto one of these, fifty-nine stories up now, I clipped myself into the

channel that runs along the middle of each fluting using a small steel hook—climbers call it a "skyhook". Secured in this way I peered into an office. No one was in at the moment. Just a desk with some papers on it, a chair, and a plant. I was disappointed—the expression of a person seeing me appear at his window was a pleasure to imagine—but it was probably for the best. The surprise wouldn't have been a healthy one.

Attached to the fluting, I paused and thought about my options for a while. My original plan, should this situation arise, was to switch over a channel on one of these flutings. At the present time, however, it didn't seem like a good idea for a number of reasons.

First of all, I didn't want to cause anyone a heart attack or to have to deal with observers behind the windows along the way. Some response from me would have been necessary and distracting. Then I thought that the police might simply bring the scaffolding around to *this* side and lower it above me, which would mean I'd have to swing over to the other side again. Even more important, I was unsure how well my devices would work on the side of the building. Where the ventilation sections divide the tower into thirds, there are small steel protrusions, decorative panels over the facade, that make the channels harder to reach; I didn't know if my devices could be maneuvered there. After mulling over these considerations, I decided to use the left-hand channel in the tower corner. Though it was just forty inches away from the one I had been using, it would still place me beyond the reach of anyone in the scaffolding.

After one last look in the office window—no one had appeared yet —I pendulumed back to the left-hand channel on the tower's corner. All the while I was hanging from the rope attached to one of my devices fifteen feet above me. I clipped a skyhook into the channel, which would hold me there and leave my arms free. Then I set to work.

THE KENNEDY ICE WALL, GLACIER PEAK.

In the late spring of 1973 I began to think about a climbing trip out west (as the weather warms, climbers' thoughts turn to the big walls in the ranges of the Tetons, Rockies, and Sierras as inevitably as the seasons turn). For me, this was not entirely practical: although my climbing skills had progressed quickly, they were still limited, and in any case I had no one to climb with out there. So I began investigating organized wilderness and mountaineering programs. Finally I picked one in the Cascades offered by the National Outdoor Leadership School; NOLS offered the most time in the mountains for the least money, five weeks for $550. To go on the trip, I'd have to take a three-week leave of absence from Ark Research on top of my meager two-week vacation, and people there warned me they couldn't guarantee I'd have a job on my return. It made no difference: climbing was far more important to me at this point.

In August, I flew out to Seattle and joined my group. There were thirteen of us, mostly men, ranging in age from seventeen to thirty-five, along with two instructors. From Bellevue, Washington, NOLS's gathering place, we were trucked to the Suiattle Roadhead. It took us two days of walking to reach the snowfields. For the next five weeks we were in the mountains, mostly above the timberline, on glaciers. We lived on rice and whole-wheat flour, other food that required no refrigeration, and dehydrated food that could be reconstituted; we ate no meat, fresh vegetables, or eggs. Carrying seventy-pound packs, we spent most of the time hiking on steep volcanic peaks. My feet ached from so much walking each day (fifteen miles or more), and there was no opportunity for them to heal. Bandage them and apply seas of moleskin to prevent chafing as I would, nothing worked, and at night they were maddeningly painful. Several in the group, because of severe blistering or staph infection, had to be evacuated by helicopter.

In some ways the trip was a disappointment; during the whole period we climbed only a couple of times. Our two guides had little enthusiasm for climbing; with only five months of climbing behind me, I was more experienced than either of them. They preferred "peak bagging," reaching the summit of some precipice by whatever route (the exact opposite of the spirit and intention of rock climbing, in which the means is far more important than the end).

Still here I was at long last in the great mountains, amid the alpine snows and glaciers, terrain I'd dreamed of since I was a boy. Ringed by soaring peaks, the snowfields reached away to the horizon, where the cloud continued the landscape of the glacier. Earth and sky came magically together. At night, when the temperature plummeted, we would sleep two to a tent on the glaciers. Though it was mid-August, the morning might bring a foot of freshly fallen snow.

During the day, apart from hiking we worked on snow and glacier techniques. We learned how to move on ice and what to

APPROACHING THE SUMMIT OF ELDORA-DO PEAK, NORTH CASCADES, WASHINGTON.

IN THE CASCADES. I'M WEARING THE GLACIER GOGGLES AND HAT AS PROTECTION AGAINST THE SUN.

do in a fall. We practiced crevasse rescue (curious about what it was like in a crevasse, I volunteered to go down in one and the others hauled me out as a drill). We practiced ice climbing. Those of us who were most adept (and eager — they usually go together) capped things off with a climb up Kennedy Glacier on Glacier Peak, a route heavily crevassed with snow bridges that features a "bergschrund," a big gap between the bottom of an ice wall and the glacier it adjoins. Crossing the begschrund, we went up the wall, which was about sixty-five degrees. The ice was very hard, the climb was long, and we ascended roped together in one continuous line of six people.

Mostly, though, we hiked day after day. Sometimes the guides would say, "Why don't we meet you in a day? You take this route" — they would point one out on a map — "and we'll go by another. We'll meet you at a campsite fifteen miles from here by the side of this river." Their way — although they would not say this — would be a shortcut. At the meeting place they'd be waiting, all smug condescension. After they'd done this a couple of times, several others and I would race — we'd *run* — carrying all that weight to beat them to the site, and we always did.

The guides' attitude provided a special incentive, but in fact I'd liked being out front, pushing myself, getting to any destination before everyone else, even as far back as when I'd been on backpacking trips in the Explorers. Some would pause, perhaps to have a smoke and lean against the trees and talk, enjoying themselves. But I'd keep going, pressing myself to see just what I could do. (Quite rightly: in a natural environment there's absolutely no reason to hurry and a great deal to be said for doing the opposite.) I wasn't looking for a race. Other people didn't really enter into it. I just liked pushing, cruising along fast, *moving*.

After leaving the Cascades, I drove down to California (pigging out at every smorgasbord place along the way, gorging myself to the astonishment of the other patrons on all the food I'd been fantasizing about for weeks) and visited Yosemite Valley for a few days. Apart from shoes, I had no climbing equipment. But I got to see El Capitan, with its famous wall, for the first time. At its base, the wall seems to lean right out over you, smooth and vast and monolithic. Walking around down there, I picked up the cast-offs of ascent groups, bits of equipment and food containers, anything that would give me a clue to what climbers had taken with them, what it had been like up there. I was absorbing it all, learning what I could, dreaming of the time when I'd tackle one of those big walls. I wasn't ready for it yet, but I knew one day I would be.

The first weekend after my return to New York, I was back at the Gunks rock climbing. The next weekend, I did a first ascent. A group had been trying all day to do a certain route that had never been climbed. Every so often this happens at a climbing area: something strikes people as an interesting problem; everyone starts talking about it, trying it; and then eventually someone does it. In this case, I was resting at the base of the cliff with my brother Paul and Jery when a climber in this group turned to me. "Hey, why don't you give it a try? It's probably a 5.7, 5.8." Had it been a 5.7, the climb could have been done in a flash. I *knew* it wasn't, but decided to try it anyway. Perhaps the climb had become a psychological barrier for these people. It was a steep, imposing, overhanging face. Sometimes when a climber doesn't know what to expect, fear will sap his strength. He becomes unwilling to extend himself to the degree he might otherwise, as he doesn't want to take a giant fall. The difficulty of the climb then lies less in the rock than in the mind, a function of self-doubt.

I tied the rope to my harness, climbed up a bit, and studied the rock. Pretty soon I figured out what hold it would be necessary to reach for. It was precipitous and the move was hard, but I knew what I had to do. Reaching, I leaned out on one hold, supported by a single foothold. But I couldn't quite get my hand on the next hold. I stretched . . . and it was then that I fell for the first time, a drop of fifteen or twenty feet.

Back down at the base, I rested for a while. Now it had become important to do this climb. It was something no one had ever done. I was an absolute unknown at the Gunks, still green. And I *knew* I could do it.

Climbing up again, I came to the "crux"—the key move—where I'd been rebuffed. Somehow this time the move was just right for me. It was the right day; I was in peak condition from all that hiking in the Cascades, and I breezed up to the ledge beyond it. The climber who had suggested I try it was beside himself. "Man! Wow! Great!" He couldn't believe it. He'd assumed I was just some young punk turkey climber (which I was). As I continued climbing I was shaking, excited about having passed the point of major difficulty. Now I was being careful, putting in a lot of protection. I'd brought a good deal of equipment because I hadn't known what to expect. Although the rest of the ascent was fearfully steep, none of the moves was as tough as the crux, and finally I reached the top, absolutely exhausted. It had been very hard work.

I tied in and belayed the other climber up. "How hard did you think it was?" he asked.

"5.8 or so," I said.

"5.8?" he said. "That's gotta be a 5.10."

"5.10!" I felt great. It would be six months before I'd try another 5.10. I was afraid, certain it had been a fluke. Unwilling to discover I couldn't do it regularly, I stayed away from anything this difficult. Still, it was a real turning point for me in climbing. It was my first first ascent. It isn't known as Willig's Way, however; it's called Shitty Mitty. The climb next to it is called Walter.

REACHING OVER THE LIP OF AN OVERHANG ON COUNTRY ROADS, A 5.10 CLIMB AT THE GUNKS.

Secured on the left-hand channel of the corner, I withdrew some spare devices and tools from my pack. Very carefully, I began to take the devices apart. Since I had no platform on which to support the instruments as I fastened them in the channel, it was a move requiring some delicacy. I had to hold both the inner portion of the device (a plate *inside* the channel) and the main part (containing the housing and the cam) outside the channel as I was screwing them together. I didn't want to drop anything, so I was going about this with all the meticulous concentration I could muster.

Even so, when I finished putting the first device in, it slipped from my hand and slid rapidly down the channel with a metallic hiss. The sound frightened me — I'd looked away for a moment — but happily the device dropped only two feet. Still on the Gibbs Ascenders, I lowered myself and retrieved it. The episode proved what I'd suspected all along: even with no load, the devices were self-locking; friction alone would engage the cam and cause it to hold.

Transferring myself to the other channel took forty-five minutes in all, a period when the crowd must have been mightily curious. Who was I? What was I doing? Was I hurt? Was I coming down or up? Was I in trouble? Was I an activist or an adventurer or just crazy? It felt very peculiar to be the focus of so much attention, to know that I was in the minds of so many strangers. I found myself imagining what my mother and father were doing at this moment, thinking about other family and friends. Wondering what was happening at Ideal Toy. Whether the people there even knew about my climb, how their day was being changed by it, if at all. And I wondered what my climbing friends would think of this. Would they respect it, or dismiss it as a stunt and me as a jerk? Certainly the climb I was doing was very different from anything one would encounter on rock.

No two ascents on a rock face are quite alike; on a cliff the demand of concentration is constant. Each move you make has an implication in terms of the move it will lead to and what this will require of you. Much of the time, climbing is like a chess problem and you must be thinking a number of steps ahead of yourself. The sequence must be correct; one misstep will place you in an untenable position.

Not only are you relying on your problem-solving ability, which is very satisfying, but you are high on a cliff, which makes everything seem all the more immediate. Once you have figured out the steps, climbing poses challenges on many other fronts: you must have physical stamina and strength; you have to conserve your strength and thus move as efficiently as you can; finally, you have to make sure that you're proceeding as safely as possible by putting in protection. There is an element of danger, though it is not so great as most people think.

Climbing challenges a person on all these fronts. It's really all-consuming.

My present climb was very different. Its most demanding aspects — figuring out a way to scale the tower, inventing and building the equipment that would enable me to do it — had preceded the climb. The sequence of steps was pretty much a given; except for my present evasive maneuver, they were all the same. It was a rote process. The danger was minimal — I had extra devices, secondary instruments, and backup safety systems; with any one of them I would have felt safe.

The climb was really only a matter of strength and ingenuity in dealing with whatever obstacles the police might throw in my way. The unknown obstacles created the tension, the things beyond my control. These apart, I could make the climb daily without the slightest qualm.

One unknown was about to arrive. Toward the end of my shift to the other channel, I saw the scaffolding coming down.

THE SCAFFOLDING
DESCENDING PAST
THE 63RD FLOOR.

Throughout the fall, winter and spring of 1973-74 I climbed at the Gunks almost every weekend, regardless of the conditions. Freezing cold, rain, snow, ice on the ledges — nothing kept me away, although when the weather was very bad I'd do easier ascents (which in extreme conditions naturally became harder). Odd as it may seem, I *liked* the foul weather; it meant new complications, different, unpredictable kinds of puzzles, and added to the whole allure of adventure.

This was the grim winter of the petroleum embargo. Since, like a good many other climbers — some came from as far as Maryland each weekend — I was practically commuting to the Gunks, the shortages might have proved a real stumbling block. But climbers have a way of transmuting hindrances into fun. The crisis atmosphere added to the excitement. Commonplace travels took on an air of unpredictability. Rationing became a game: on the day they were eligible to buy gas, those with odd-numbered plates would go fill up, return to the cliffs, siphon the gas into the tank of an even-numbered car, then return to the station and fill up again (a ploy not limited, I suspect, to climbers). I traded in my van for a VW Squareback, which was economical on gas and had room to sleep comfortably in the back, packed an extra five-gallon tank, and the climbing went on.

Before my trip to the Cascades, I'd been climbing on a steady basis with Peter Rossi, an amiable, easy-going climber whom I'd met at the Gunks. Ordinarily, climbers try to hook up with a regular partner, someone with whom they share similar climbing tastes, abilities, and ambitions. Some climbers may only want to do one or two ascents a day, then relax and hang around the cliffs. To them, the ambience and talk may be as enjoyable as what happens on the rock. Others want only to climb; they get up early and all day long follow one ascent with another (usually I'm this way, although when I'm alone I may be more casual about it).

My first climb with Peter did not exactly suggest a matched brace of temperaments. One hundred feet up on the rock, he paused to inquire, "By the way, do you play bridge?" "*Bridge?*" I asked. Up on a cliff, an activity so sedentary and *flat* seemed unimaginable to me. "What're you talking about? We're *climbing.* How could you even think of bridge?" But Peter was a fanatical player and eventually gave up climbing to concentrate on the tournament circuit. Long before he did this, however, it had become clear that our interests were diverging. While Peter was more conservative and casual about climbing, I found myself driven to try harder and harder things, even if it meant falling more often; moreover, I wanted to climb as much as possible. Because of this, I began pairing up that spring with Steve Matous, an aggressive, energetic climber whose enthusiasm for the sport was a match for my own (four years later, Steve would climb Angel's Landing in

STEVE MATOUS, AT RAGGED MOUNTAIN IN CONNECTICUT. NOTE THE THREE POINTS OF PROTECTION THROUGH WHICH THE ROPE PASSES.

Utah with me for ABC).

Evenings, I'd hang out with other climbers at Emile's, a German place about a half-mile from the cliffs. There were about ten of us "hard men," as we were called. We were the ones who were always up there, in any conditions, doing extreme climbing. It was a congenial group—the first one in which I'd ever really felt comfortable—and we had a lot to share. Down at Emile's, pleasantly tired and buoyant with camaraderie, we'd laugh a lot, drink, and trade horror stories about what had happened up on the cliffs—or, more to the point, what might have happened; how we'd almost died, or how scared we'd been on climbs, or how good we'd felt after having done them. Among these climbers there was no hesitancy to admit or speak of fear. Quite the opposite. They would exaggerate their fears, dramatize them, perhaps to make what they wanted to say acceptable. It was a way, perhaps, of talking about their achievements without seeming overbearing.

These men had a few traits in common. They tended to be withdrawn, loners; most were single or divorced. Climbing seemed to have eclipsed the other things in their lives; they spent so much time climbing that relationships became difficult to sustain. Whether this situation is a product of the activity or of the temperament that precedes it and makes climbing so appealing, I couldn't say. My own relationship at that time with a girl certainly suffered (and finally ended) because climbing was all I wanted to do. On weekends, I was never around. I was unavailable for parties; I never saw friends; my interest in work diminished. As soon as possible on Fridays, I'd be on my way back up to the Gunks. For callers, my parents developed an automatic mock-suffering response. "He's *climbing*, of course." It was not the sort of life likely to develop anything besides climbing skills.

The way climbers speak of their fears is connected to a larger courtesy, a mutual support system, often encountered among them. Climbers are extravagant in their praise for boldness on the rocks. They're always complimenting each other. When someone is out on a lead, in a position that is particularly scary or difficult and perhaps having trouble, they will try to give him every kind of encouragement. They want to see him make it; if he doesn't and *you* do it with ease, guilt sets in as if you'd shown him up, bruised his ego. It goes back to the centrality of the idea that there are no winners or losers in climbing. Care must be taken, and so you say: "Wow, that was unbelievable! I don't know how I made it. *Really* hard moves. I just must've had a good day." Or: "Luckily, I was rested, I'm sure you could've done it if you hadn't had to work the moves out. Watching you, I figured out how it might go a little better." Which might even be true.

There is an unusual relationship between two climbers on an ascent. You're out there on the rock, alone. But you're connected by a rope, from which unless you fall you're not getting any sustenance or support (except perhaps an indirect psychological one). But it is there. The other person is there in case you need him. You have entrusted your lives to each other. You don't *have* to have him there. It is possible to climb alone. But it is much more dangerous.

Despite this (and sometimes because of it), the freedom of solo climbing is especially appealing. You can move very smoothly. You don't have to bother with stopping every rope length to bring the other climber up. There is a greater continuity to it, a nicer flow. You are more vulnerable, and every element of the climb is intensified. The price that you might have to pay for each move is a lot higher.

In a game like tennis, if you go out on the court and shuffle around dispiritedly, the worst the play will be is stultifying. But in climbing, the risk is death and it is ever present and always at its greatest when you are climbing alone. There is no such thing as a shuffle; you fall or do not get up the rock. Even on easy climbs, the risk is the same. If you are one hundred feet up and you fall, the result is not in doubt.

Putting your self on the line like this is uniquely and undeniably exciting. But it is a measured risk, not simple thrill seeking. When I climb without the protection of another person I'll do an easier climb than I would ordinarily—one on which I won't get too frightened. I'm always willing to back down if I'm on something too difficult. Alone, I'm much more conservative in my decisions.

Sometimes I'll climb alone because I *am* alone, and it is that or nothing. Sometimes I do it as therapy. If something is troubling me, often I won't want to be with anyone else. I'll go out on my own and do some very easy things, just cruising around really. Once I'm moving along the rock I'll start to feel better. Other things will slip away as I think about the rock. My confidence will begin to grow and soon I'll be ready to try something harder, perhaps with someone else.

Even when solo climbing, extending myself occasionally becomes irresistible, although I try not to do it often. I'll find myself up on some wall with a hard move to make, and I'll reason, Here I am on some pretty good holds. Perhaps I'll reach up to test the holds, work out the sequence, then come back down. Usually at this point I'll be starting to get sweaty, as fear threads its insistent way into my thoughts, and decide: I'll stay on this ledge here, just relax, and then I'll take another look around. Then I might go a little higher and try a move. I'll look and see the good hold, higher up, that I'm going for, and think: Boy, just let me get to that. But I'll be a little too shaky now. I won't feel secure where I am and so I'll retreat a bit, rest, and think about it. What am I doing up there? How come I'm not climbing with someone, doing this safely? Why do I extend myself like this?

I'll look down from the gut-wrenching height and think, Oh, Jesus, if I fall ... My mind will be racing: I wonder if I could direct my fall over to that tree and have the branches break it. Which is idiotic: I have no chance of directing myself anywhere. At an altitude of a thousand feet, a climber might possibly use the wind, but never at a hundred. Still these calculations creep in, along with bizarre morbid thoughts: If it happens, I wonder where I'll land. I wonder what it'll be like. Will my leg bones go right through my hips?

At a certain point, a decision must be made. Sometimes I'll just go for it, in pure concentration. Then falling becomes unreal, no longer a possibility. Occasionally I'll freak out, decide it's crazy, and climb off to an easier section. It all depends on my psychological disposition. If I'm feeling good and I'm comfortable on the rock, I'm less apt to become unnerved. If, on the other hand, I've had a bad week and my attitude is poor, chances are that I'll back down. On certain days, I won't even start a solo climb. (Overcoming the urge to do a climb can be an accomplishment in itself; to admit that an ascent is at a given moment beyond your abilities and would be foolhardy is only common sense).

I've gone back to try a solo climb ten times, backing down again and again, until eventually one day I do it. These returns to a difficult spot are a way of mentally preparing yourself (a lesson that was to serve me well in my World Trade Center climb). There is much to prepare: you have to work out the successive holds and memorize the face of the rock. The idea here, as in other climbing, is to break the ascent down into smaller sections. The key to solo climbing, as for a tightrope walker who uses no net, is to know yourself very, very well; to know what your exact limits are and when you are pushing them. It is the kind of lesson that climbing teaches.

Throughout that year, my climbing skills steadily improved. In the summer, I made a trip out to the Grand Tetons. After I returned, a number of things soon changed.

As the scaffolding came down, I saw that two cops were on it. One, I'd soon learn, was a New York City policeman named Dewitt Allen, the other, Glenn Kildare, was with the Port Authority police.

When they drew within shouting distance, Allen called to me: "What're you, *crazy?*" His tone was jocular—indulgent rather than angry.

"Not really," I called back. "But you might think I am." Might?

The scaffolding stopped, now level with me. "We got to stop meeting like this," Dewitt said. "My wife is getting annoyed." We all laughed. He was humoring me, obviously—for all he knew I was a lunatic —but I was relieved he was taking a light approach. At least there would be no unpleasantness to mar the climb.

Safely beyond their reach, I presented my case. This wasn't a spur-of-the-moment prank, I told them, but something I'd been planning for a long, long time. "I know you think I'm crazy and probably everyone else does, but this is something I've worked on for a year. I developed these devices. I went through a lot of different design changes. "Here"—I showed them—"this is how they work." I slid one up the channel and demonstrated its locking action.

"I'm really pretty comfortable up here," I assured them. "I'm used to heights. And unusual as this whole thing might seem to be, I'm gonna make it."

Dewitt looked at me for a moment, then smiled. He had a walkie-talkie that he was using to talk to his sergeant in the Emergency Services, a division of the police force specializing in tricky rescue operations—talking potential suicides down off bridges (or maniacs off the walls of skyscrapers). Now he spoke into it. "Sarge," he said, "this guy sounds like he's okay. He knows what he's doing. He's an experienced climber and he's making his way up okay. He seems to be all right. Should I let him keep going?"

Let him? What was his choice? My strategic position was excellent. Even if I'd been in the right-hand channel, I would have been able to evade them. Dewitt, who was closer to me, would have had to lean way out; in response, I could simply have swung over in the opposite direction. This was academic, as neither of the policemen was *about* to do that. They were clipped and tied to the edge of that scaffolding. They were out of their element. I was in mine.

Over the radio I heard the sergeant suggest I hitch a ride in the scaffolding. "Do you want to swing over into this thing?" Dewitt asked me.

"No, thanks," I answered. "I wouldn't want to risk a tricky maneuver like that up here. I feel safer just climbing." There was nothing tricky about it; I could easily have swung over to them. But I wasn't about to tell *them* that.

They discussed their options a bit more.

"I'd hate to be in that thing you guys are in." I said.

"Don't say that!" Dewitt grabbed onto the railing in mock terror. Gaining my confidence was a basic objective in their kind of work, but I admired his cool approach all the same. I sat back in my harness as we talked. The breeze blew steadily, and it was chilly now that I was not climbing. The two rivers were shining brightly in the sun. It was absolutely cloudless, without haze. The distant ocean was the pale blue of the morning sky. The towers of the financial district rose up all around me. Seen from the side above or high up, they seem even more astonishing than on the ground; beside them, one has an even greater feeling of their mass.

"How about a safety line, at least?" asked Glenn Kildare, the Port Authority policeman.

"No, I don't want a safety line. I want to do it all on my own."

They understood, I think. At least, neither of them tried to push it. "All right, we'll just ride up with him." Dewitt finally told his sergeant. And that was that. All they could do now was to settle back and enjoy the ride.

At this point, I decided to return to the right hand channel. The devices I'd been using there—the ones that had gotten me up this far— had been worn in, and were working much more smoothly than the fresh ones I'd installed in the left channel (the right ones were hard enough on my hands, as it was). If Dewitt and Glenn suddenly changed their minds about not interfering, I could always evade them. Having decided this, I meticulously disassembled the devices in the left channel, put the instruments and tools back in my pack, and pendulumed over to the right channel. After transferring my stirrups and slings to the devices once more, I removed the Gibbs Ascenders and began recoiling the rope.

TALKING THINGS OVER. I'M STILL IN THE LEFT-HAND CHANNEL.

Two important things happened when I returned from the Tetons in the fall of 1974. The first was that I developed a problem with my back that was serious enough that I thought I'd never climb again.

It seemed to have begun with a slight shoulder injury that I received on a climb in early October. I was making a difficult 5.10 move, straining for a hold, when I heard a tearing sound in my shoulder. A partial dislocation had occurred, requiring me to wear my arm in a sling for a couple of weeks. Then, mysteriously, my back began hurting. I looked for causes: not long before, I'd been moving heavy machinery at Ark—perhaps this was it. The only other possible episode I could dredge up was a thirty-foot fall I'd taken while climbing a few weeks earlier. It was no big deal: I was fifteen feet past my last point of protection when my foot slid off the rock; I fell, thought nothing of it, and finished the climb.

Whatever the cause, my back hurt like hell. In all, I visited four orthopedic surgeons. The first team diagnosed it as a sprain and suggested bed rest. Though I tried it for a few weeks, the condition grew worse. Then two other doctors (who also decided my problem was a sprained back) prescribed Valium, which was useless, and recommended a corset; but immobility only increased the pain. This nonsense went on for six or eight months, during which time I couldn't even stand up comfortably.

Even if the remedy was problematical, at least one thing appeared clear: my climbing days seemed to be over. Not only was climbing painful and frustrating now—as a couple of days at the Gunks had shown me—but I was afraid it would make my back worse. The choice, given what the doctors were saying, appeared to be between giving up climbing or becoming an invalid.

For over a year and a half, climbing had been what I was about, and now for a while the bottom dropped out of things. But what could I do? I had no alternative except to resign myself to the change, and eventually other things began to absorb my attention. Particularly working with stained-glass, of all things, in which I took a course that winter. Right away, I started on ambitious projects, complex designs, terrariums, lamps.

Meantime, someone at Ark suggested I try a chiropractor for my back. After wasted months of shuttling between ineffective diagnosticians, I had finally found the answer. With a steady regimen of treatments, my back improved. The chiropractor had other good news for me: climbing, in all likelihood, had nothing to do with the pain; he thought its source might be a congenital deformity in my back. What's more, rest and immobility were about the worst things for it. As long as I flexed my spine, my back wouldn't hurt. And when I started climbing again, I discovered my back actually felt better for it. So I was back in business.

In the interim, however, I'd picked up a valuable lesson, largely through my interest in stained glass. Life didn't begin and end with climbing. Without it I could still be happy. I'd missed it; now it played a big part in my life again; but it was no longer central to what I was doing. Becoming a climber was the biggest boost I've ever had, but this was certainly a healthier perspective.

Another thing kept me from spending a lot of time on the cliffs. After I returned from the Tetons, I went back to college. For some time I'd been restless in my job at Ark, and I decided to try something else. As my mother was still working at St. John's University, the tuition there would be free, and now I decided to have another go at it.

At first, I studied accounting. *Accounting?* Well, for a while I was being practical. It seemed like a lucrative field, even a challenging one—at least I enjoyed doing my tax returns— but then my truer nature asserted itself. I thought, What a drag sitting at a desk all day, and switched to environmental studies simply because it was something that I liked. At the time, I had vague ideas it might lead to a job with the Environmental Protection Agency.

What intrigued me particularly was environmental philosophy, a subject that addresses the questions involved in how we deal with the environment—balancing long-term benefits, for example, with short-term exploitation. The issues had concerned me since I was a boy, as I watched the woods disappear around my aunt's house on Long Island, as the natural world slipped farther and farther away. These questions *still* concern me. How, when resources are finite, can we squander them as if there could be no end? Surely it makes more sense to consider the physical world as an extension of our own bodies; we're no less dependent on it. And how long can we ignore the irreversibly destructive effects of the technology of growth?

Even now, for example, swamps are being used for handy dumps or even more commonly packed with landfill to make room for houses. This despite the fact that much of the nourishment for the oceans comes out of these swamps and estuaries; if all of them were filled in, the oceans would die. In this country, 30 percent of all marine marshes have already been filled.

What about all the industrial wastes, the toxic effluents, the chemicals, live explosives, garbage, and sewage that are still poured into the sea? In the Atlantic, near the buoy where the Ambrose Light Ship was once moored, is an area called The Dead Sea. It is a dumping ground for sewage sludge and thus rife with the pathogens that derive from human wastes—a fertile breeding place for encephalitis and hepatitis. As fish swim through this area, their fins disintegrate; many die. Is *this* where we propose to find new sources of food? Simple objections, often stated; but have they led us to go about things more responsibly?

For so long, people have acted to achieve a short-term effect without any sense of its implications. For many years when engineers constructed jetties, for example, they didn't understand the workings of the littoral drift. The shorelines of barrier beaches are highly dynamic. Sand is constantly shifting from north to south. Beaches erode and then build up again. Jetties *will* divert the littoral drift out and sand will accumulate in a given spot. But for miles down the coast, once that flow is diverted the drift will not return and those beaches will erode away. For us to suppose we can shape a force so elemental is simple arrogance.

In environmental studies, my courses had the immediacy of what were (for me) natural preoccupations. Outside this area, my favorite subjects were theology and philosophy. I liked grappling with the big, timeless questions: What is man? What is the purpose of life? What is happiness? What are values? It was at this level that I wanted to engage people. Small talk made me impatient. I wanted to know how they *felt* about things.

A key influence at this time was a professor named Father Simms, who taught a course in western civilization. His pet bugaboo was what he called "mass man," and the mass mentality that now seems so prevalent. He deplored people's willingness, even anxiousness, to surrender their identities to that of the herd, to fall into comfortable fads, fashionable, *expected*, conventional modes of behavior. Isn't it this frame of mind that most advertising cannily taps these days? Father Simms had a high estimation of man, and he stretched our minds to accommodate it. (As he lectured, the same cigarette would make an interminable, suspenseful path from his pack as his attention was successively ambushed by arresting points; it might take a whole period for the cigarette to find the completion of a match.) Man, he believed, is more than a cog or a wheel or a malleable belt on a machine constantly being manipulated. He saw him as free-thinking, able to determine what he can do with himself, and, because of this, ultimately responsible for himself. Character was the key to history, Father Simms believed, and he reduced the sweep of events to the most basic terms: the Church of England being founded because the Pope wouldn't give Henry VIII a divorce; a religion and the course of history changed because of the simple outsized appetites of a single petulant man. What Father Simms was saying could hardly have struck a more responsive chord in me.

At St. John's I crammed about three years' work into two (two years at a time, I'd learned, was about all I was good for), taking classes right through the summer. During this period I had little time to climb. My climbing diary tells me that in my second year at St. John's I went up to the Gunks only twice during the whole fall and spring, once on the fourth of November and again on February 27. Then in May 1976, I had a month off before the next term began, and when Bill Beck, a climbing acquaintance from New Hampshire, happened to mention that he was looking for company for a trip to Yosemite, I said right away that I'd go. I hadn't had any hard, sustained climbing for almost two years. It was time.

Once I'd recoiled the rope and had all my equipment stowed away in my pack, I began climbing again. Pushing. Stepping up, side to side. Dewitt and Glenn, on the scaffolding, stayed with me, chatting, ascending a floor or two at a time. By now it was about eight-thirty, and I was at the sixtieth floor.

"Want us to carry your pack for you?" one of them asked.

"No, I don't mind carrying it," I told them. "I want to be self-sufficient." In other words, I wanted the climb to be as if they weren't there. I was making good progress now. They seemed surprised at how quickly I could move.

Along the way, we introduced ourselves, almost as an afterthought. "I was the guy yelling and screaming at you down there," Glenn Kildare told me. It seemed like days ago. "How come you didn't listen to me?" He sounded a little hurt.

"This is the only chance I've got," I said. "I couldn't. I couldn't come down. I knew I could climb all the way to the top even though you told me it wasn't possible."

"Yeah," he answered a bit sheepishly, "I was really upset." Upset? He was completely *gonzo*. "I was excited." Now he was excited in a different way, obviously taken up in the exhilaration of the climb. Both of them were.

A pack of helicopters came swarming in from the direction of the Brooklyn Bridge. Within moments, there were six or eight of them there, buzzing around like bees in a hive, jockeying for position. I could see the TV cameramen and still photographers inside, shooting away. One chopper would hover in close, get its footage, and swing out. Then the next one would edge in, and its cameras would roll. I could look right into the faces of those within—a peculiar exchange at such a height in such circumstances—as they watched from behind their windows. I particularly remember staring right into the camera of a *Daily News* photographer; these helicopters seemed like pursuit ships, and I wanted to look my antagonists straight in the eye. I stared at them, unsmiling. All morning I'd been the object of so much curiosity that somehow now I felt the tables were briefly turned as these newspeople, in their hectic mission, became the object of mine.

The cops, meanwhile, were frantically waving off the choppers, screaming at them to "get away!" They thought it was very dangerous. The helicopter that the *Daily News* had hired was at one point no more than a hundred feet away (I imagined the photographer peeling bills off an enormous wad as he urged the pilot closer and closer). The pilots were highly skilled and held their crafts steady in the stiff wind, but I suppose a sudden gust might have buffeted one against the tower. Completely ignoring the cops on the scaffolding, these latter-day barnstormers hovered there for ten or fifteen minutes, swooping in and out over the Hudson, passing close to one another, as they returned again and again for more pictures. Finally a police helicopter appeared and flew around the other choppers like an exacerbated mother hen, shooing them away and doubtless threatening them with untold grief. As abruptly as they had arrived, they buzzed away in the direction from which they had come. What they were doing was absolutely against the law. My own position, on the other hand, was of course beyond reproach.

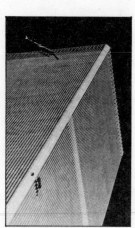

A HELICOPTER AR-RIVES.

The trip to Yosemite didn't get off to a promising start. On the day we were to leave, my traveling companion, Bill Beck, never showed up (we were planning to drive out in his old VW bus). For several days, as the excitement of the trip dribbled away, I waited, packed and waiflike, as my family looked on sympathetically. Finally, on the third day Bill called; he'd lost his job at the Goddard Space Research Center in New Hampshire, he reported apologetically. The next day he arrived, and after replacing the rear brakes on his bus (among other repairs) we were on our way. At least until Laramie, Wyoming — we'd stopped to visit my brother Steve, who was attending the university there — where the transmission on Bill's bus gave up the ghost.

We were lucky. Not only was Dr. Don's Bug Hospital just a few steps down the road, but — providence was really pulling strings here — Dr. Don had a VW bus offering all those parts that Bill's needed (everything but the engine and tires). Dr. Don was in a mood to deal. A bargain was rapidly struck, and Bill's engine and tires were transferred. We spent the night installing the custom interior touches from Bill's old bus in his new(er) one And the next day we set out again.

In Yosemite at last, I was anxious to climb. I wanted to test myself on one of the famous big walls there: El Capitan, Sentinel Rock, or Half Dome. In every way I was ready for it now. Except for one thing: a partner. The day after we arrived, Bill, Gail — a friend of Bill's who had joined us in Salt Lake City — and I did do one long, eighteen-pitch ascent called Royal Arches; it was a 5.6 climb with two 5.9 options, which I took alone. Gail was slow and unsure on the rock. By the time we finished the climb, it was dark and had turned cold, and we had to walk until early morning to reach our campsite in the valley — at Sunnyside Campground (or "Camp 4," as the climbers call it), where all the climbers seem to stay. After this, bummed out about his job and distracted by Gail's company, Bill lost interest in climbing.

Happily, I ran into Michael Hartrich, a friend and very experienced climber and instructor from New Hampshire. Mike has a wry sense of humor and a dry streak of malice that make him diverting company. Ordinarily he would have been a fine partner for an ambitious ascent, but Mike's frame of mind wasn't any too happy either. In the past few weeks he'd been rebuffed twice by bad weather on El Capitan, once when he'd been two thirds of the way up. Mike was also feeling the effects of a ninety-foot fall he'd taken the week before. Aside from some rope burns and scrapes he was all right, but he was fed up, worn out. His hands were battered; he'd been out there too long, he said. To my disappointment, he'd lost interest in climbing anything big. Still, we did a lot of very difficult, shorter climbs together. Lunatic Fringe was one ascent we did in this period.

MIKE HARTRICH, CRACK CLIMBING ON ANATHEMA, A 5.10 ASCENT IN YOSEMITE VALLEY. HIS FEET ARE FRICTIONED AGAINST THE ROCK.

It felt wonderful to be doing this kind of demanding technical climbing again. And I also had a pleasant time relaxing in the valley, tubing one day with Bill, Gail, and Mike on the fast chilly waters of the Merced River, talking, camping, and — naturally — living on peanut butter.

Peanut butter is the climber's mainstay, the steady backbone of his diet. It's cheap — important as climbers *never* have any money (no wonder, they're always climbing) — it has plenty of protein, it's convenient, and it doesn't require refrigeration (sardines and tuna fish are also popular for these reasons, though not in a class with peanut butter). Now, when I say "peanut butter," I don't mean Skippy. I mean the kind available in health-food stores, the kind that has some grain to it. With supermarket peanut butter — why, you might as well be eating margarine! But grainy, thick, oily, almost liquid peanut butter is another story. Add honey, and it deserves a French name. Bananas and bacon complement and extend the flavor as a fine sauce might. My personal favorite is peanut butter with lettuce, American cheese, mayonnaise, and — yes — potato chips, a climber's club sandwich.

Peanut butter has its many champions, but I've never met a more passionate exponent of it than Mike Hartrich. He is — why mince words? — a total peanut butter freak, always alert for (as he puts it) new "vehicles." Walking along a trail one day, Mike stopped to pick up a small especially flat rock. "I've just discovered another vehicle for peanut butter," he announced. Tortilla chips were another discovery of this period.

In the evenings, Mike and I — along with many other climbers — would go over to the plush Yosemite Lodge across the road from Camp 4. After burrowing in the wastebaskets, we'd sit in the lobby's comfortable chairs reading the newspapers discarded by guests. (Scrounging is typical behavior for climbers, who are generally unacceptable types; in the slack spring season, the hotel management is usually indulgent.) In one paper, I found a recipe for peanut butter chiffon pie — another vehicle! — which I passed along to Mike. The possibilities for peanut butter are, it seems, inexhaustible.

After about three weeks at Yosemite, Bill Beck, Mike, John Powell (an English climber we'd met out there), and I drove to Mount Whitney, in the Sierra Nevada of eastern California. We planned to climb Keeler Needle, a dramatic 3000-foot spire that sticks up nearly vertically from the mountain. From Bishop, California, the road went steeply up Mount Whitney's flank to 8000 feet, where we left the bus. Our map of the area was poor; as Bill, who has a degree in geography (at Goddard, his job had been interpreting satellite photos), and Mike squabbled about our route — John and I stayed out of it — we hiked up to 12,000 feet, carrying all our climbing and camping gear, where we established a base camp.

It was very cold, and we were all a little lethargic; everyone had headaches from the altitude but me. (Oddly, I've never had one, or a tooth- or earache, for that matter; or perhaps I've *always* had one and can't tell the difference.) Then in the late afternoon, it grew seriously cold, and the wind began to blow. We built a small stone shelter for protection. With all of us in there it was cramped and difficult to sleep, and we passed most of the night playing word games as the wind howled outside. The next morning we rose, still lethargic, and got our equipment together. The plan was to do the climb in two teams (less cumbersome than a single party of four — less rope, less crowded on the belay ledges, and less equipment to haul, among other considerations). Mike and John were going to start first, and then that night or the next morning, Bill and I would follow. Accordingly, Mike and John went up ahead to reconnoiter the area and choose a route; three hours later, they were back, disgusted, at the campsite. We were in the wrong valley, or, as it's technically called, the wrong "cirque" — the hollow between vertical ridges (arretes) on the mountain wall. To reach Keeler Needle, we'd have to rappel and climb down 1000 feet over loose, broken rock, then hike a couple of miles.

JOHN POWELL AND MIKE HARTRICH (*RIGHT*), IN THE SHELTER ON MT. WHITNEY.

The hell with it, we decided. We were tired anyway. We'd simply climb to the summit of Mount Whitney by what's called the "old ladies' route," a long, uncomplicated hike up to nearly 15,000 feet, the highest point in the continental United States. It was very beautiful at that altitude, but by this time Mike and Bill had horrible headaches and John hadn't felt well enough to make the climb at all. There is nothing to take for a mountain headache; it comes from ascending too rapidly and the only remedy is to wait until you become accustomed to the height or to descend to a lower altitude. So we started down. At 12,000 feet, Mike and Bill paused to spend the night, not feeling well enough to continue. Impatient to get it over with and unwilling to break the pleasurable momentum that I'd built up, I kept going in the dark until I reached the bus.

The next day when Mike and Bill came down, we set off back east, by way of Death Valley. What can compare with a cross-country road trip with friends? This time, we took the southern route along Interstate 40. In Albuquerque, New Mexico, we lent John Powell some money — for weeks he'd carried scrounging to new limits — and he blew it on a bottle of wine for us, the cheapest he could find. In Texas, a thunderstorm spliced with lightning stayed right ahead of us for hundreds of miles. Late at night in Louisiana, as I was driving and John and Bill lay sleeping in the back, Mike, restless for some action, poured gasoline in a metal cup and lighted it, screaming "Bill! John! The car is on fire!" Startled, Bill awoke, saw a flame in the front seat, and began yelling, "Holy shit!" to Mike's vast pleasure. At an Arkansas rest stop, not having showered in a week (Mike, particularly rank, claimed two), we washed — bathed almost — in sinks.

In West Virginia, we stopped to climb at Seneca Rocks. The area is lovely with high, sawtooth hills and lush vegetation, the

98

WASHINGTON
SQUARE PARK, WITH
THE WORLD TRADE
CENTER IN THE
BACKGROUND. THIS
WAS TAKEN ON THE
DAY OF SIGHTSEEING
WITH MIKE AND
JOHN.

result of a notably moist climate. Tired from the trip, we did only two ascents on that cloudy day. I used a wonderful old pay phone to call home from there that had to be cranked; you held the receiver to the ear and spoke into a microphone on the box. Twenty-four hours later, after leaving the others at Bill's parents' house near Philadelphia, I was back in Queens.

Two days afterward, Mike and John joined me in New York for a short visit. We were in Washington Square Park sightseeing when I pointed out the Twin Towers to them. "Those are the famous buildings that Philippe Petit walked between and someone else parachuted off," I told them. "One of these days someone is probably going to climb it," I said. "It's the only thing left to do." It was the first time the thought had occurred to me. From that time on, I was taken with the idea of the climb.

MIKE HARTRICH
CLIMBING THE OLD
LADIES' ROUTE UP
MT. WHITNEY.

From the scaffolding, the two cops were telling me how I was going to be a star. "You're going to be really famous. You wouldn't believe the reaction to this thing already. The newspapers are down there," they were saying. "Radio, TV. *Everybody*. You're going to be a real hero. You're going to be a millionaire." They stopped only a bit short of the presidency. Just circumspect, I guess.

A few helicopters were one thing, but all this seemed pretty silly to me. "Nah, I doubt it," I told them. I had absolutely no conception of or reason to expect either the dimension or the tenor of the reaction the climb was receiving. "I didn't do it for that, you know," I added. "It doesn't matter if that happens or not."

They waved away my reservations. "You'll see. You'll be a hero. You'll be on all the talk shows, Johnny Carson and all that." Nirvana, in a word. "C'mon," I said. All that really couldn't have seemed more remote or unimportant. I stopped for a sip of water—my mouth was dry almost all the time now—and looked down at the crowds below. I'd climbed a story or two above my companions, and as I paused they brought the scaffolding up to me.

"Don't worry about any criminal charges. They'll all be dropped," Dewitt said. Both of them seemed certain of it, having had an opportunity gauge the temper of the response below, and I suppose from having seen this kind of thing occur on a smaller scale.

"Well, that remains to be seen," I said. "I really don't know." Actually, I told them, I wasn't worried about any charges. The climb was exciting enough that I'd be willing to pay any price for it. Given all the commotion, however, it seemed likely I'd have to pay *something*.

Their buoyancy was unshakable. "You'll come out of this better than before it happened," they assured me. I couldn't think about it and at this moment had no inclination to. Now I had an idea that was a good deal more immediate. My hands had become very raw from hitting the devices and had blistered badly. I showed them to the cops and, as I went along, explained what I was doing. Taking off my pack, I removed two of the instruments I'd first constructed to get up the building (later, because I was so pleased with my second design, I relegated these to a backup, safety position). As a precaution, I attached these devices to a sling, using a carabiner; that way, if I dropped them they wouldn't fall.

As I stepped up, I used one as a little hammer to get the climbing devices moving along the track. What a difference! Reaching an intersection in the panels, I also used the device to straighten the channel ends that were out of alignment. Now I stood a chance of finishing the climb with my palms intact. I looked up. More than halfway, I figured. Forty-five stories to go. Once again, I started climbing in earnest.

PHILIPPE PETIT.

I certainly wasn't the first to have thought of climbing the World Trade Center. Some months before, in the "Dream Ascents" section of *Ascent*, a mountaineering journal published by the Sierra Club, I'd seen an illustration of a climber on the Center's wall. In the drawing, the climber appeared huge, dwarfing the tower — perhaps by dint of sheer guts! Another reference, of which I was unaware at the time of my climb, had appeared in *The Climber's Source Book*, where scaling the World Trade Center was described as one of the last great mountaineering feats. Still closer to home was a conversation Jery and I had had one day that fall with a salesman at Eastern Mountain Sports. We were talking about the Unisphere film, then in progress, when he happened to mention that some friends of his were planning to climb the World Trade Center, using — of all things — telescoping chinning bars between the columns. Jery and I looked at each other saying nothing. Actually, since the climb, a number of others have told me they'd considered attempting the ascent, too.

I don't doubt it; tackling a skyscraper is hardly an unusual thing for a climber to think about. The fact is that even though the activity has only recently been given a fashionable name, "buildering," people have been scampering up structures for years, probably for as long as others have been constructing them. Philippe Petit, who walked between the Twin Towers on a wire, once told me that he cannot look at two high adjacent structures without thinking of walking between them. Climbers think of climbing in a similar way; in a cliff or a tower they see a problem and a challenge, and their thoughts turn inevitably toward discovering a solution. Whether the objects of the climbers' attention are the products of nature or of technology, the invitation to their skill and ingenuity is the same.

Now that I had the idea, how would I go about it? My first notion was to use suction cups on the windows. Not as farfetched as it sounds: there are large ones, employed in connection with little pumps that evacuate the air within, that can support a weight of 500 pounds; these are used in the transport of glass. But what if the windows were dirty or filmy? My knowledge of the equipment was too limited even to guess.

A few days after the Washington Square Park outing, I discussed the idea with Jery Hewitt. We've known each other since high school; while at Farmingdale, each day we drove out to college together and have been close friends since. When meeting girls in those days we had a set line, a shared joke — "Hi, we're two dull guys" — which made light of our self-consciousness (and pride) about not enjoying the mainstream kicks of others our age. We liked blues and jazz rather than rock, had no use for drugs, like to generate our own excitement; it was a bond between us. Jery is adventurous, animated, high spirited, and independent; he gave up a promising career in the food business to become a stunt man. This was a lean period for him; for two years he'd been trying, without much success, to break into the film business. But he stuck to it, determinedly perfecting and extending his range of "gags." Now, happily, he's an accomplished professional who works regularly.

If my first thoughts were of climbing the building, my next ones were of asking Jery to join me. I wanted to share it with him, the anxiety and excitement of the preparation and of course the experience itself. Two people could help and reinforce each other, psychologically and physically. During both stages, we'd be able to talk about it, support each other. And I thought this would be a strong credit for Jery's work; perhaps even the breakthrough he needed. "It sounds good," Jery said when I asked him. "I'd like to do it." And that was it. Later he'd change his mind. But now, and in fact during most of the preparation, the plan was for two people to make the ascent.

JERY EXECUTING A
FALLING GAG.

Suction cups might well have worked, but it seemed likely to me that a superior mechanical solution lay waiting to be discovered. I decided to have a look at the building and see exactly what I was up against. Two weeks later, on a Friday evening in mid-June, I went down there. My first visit to the Twin Towers coincided with my first outing with Randy Zeidberg; we were on our way to the Gunks together. (It wasn't a date. Although I'd known Randy casually for awhile—she'd been climbing at the Gunks longer than I—she was seeing someone else at the time, and it would be several months before we'd become romantically involved.) Would she mind, I asked her in the car, if we stopped off at the World Trade Center on our way? I was thinking of climbing it, I told her. Randy's eyes didn't shift nervously, figuring an escape route from my car. She didn't seem astonished. She didn't swoon at my hardy (verbal) dering-do. Climbers are *always* talking about climbing things, as I've suggested, and so she simply said with interest, "Sure, let's go down there," and we did.

As soon as I looked at the towers I noticed the corners. It was the channels that caught my attention, channels that went all the way from the very bottom of each building to the top. This was true *only* at the corners; on the sides of the buildings, because of the lobby design, the channels didn't begin until the third story. Once I saw this continuous feature, I immediately became excited and thoughts of such cumbersome unsure methods of ascent as suction cups were discarded. These channels looked good and strong; they were made in ten-foot sections of stainless steel, each attached by five screws. I took a six-inch ruler that I carried in the car, measured the channel, made a quick sketch on a pad I'd brought, and right away had an idea for a device that I thought would work.

Then we drove up to the Gunks. I talked about the climb halfway upstate. I hadn't expected the tower to be so vulnerable, that a practical solution would present itself so quickly. Visiting the building had thoroughly psyched me. It had turned an idea into an exact plan, and now my enthusiasm was keen.

Back at home I spent about a week refining my design, then translating it into a working drawing with precise dimensions from which a model might be tooled. When I was ready, I went to Ark Research—although I hadn't worked there in more than a year, I'd kept in touch with people there—and asked Bob Bidwell, my former boss, if I might use the machining equipment. I told him, as I told everyone there with the exception of my good friend Jim Tinguely and a couple of others, that I was working on an idea for a safety device for window washers.

A little circumspection seemed to be called for; permission to use Ark's equipment was key to the climb. Without it, I'd have had no alternative but to pay to have my design executed— expensive work I could never have afforded. In addition, Bob tended toward the paternal, and I was concerned that he might worry about me. (This was the same thing I told my parents; my zeal for the project was such that I couldn't resist saying *something*, but I didn't want to reveal my true plans—not yet.) Bob said to go ahead, by all means; as long as I wasn't in the way I was free to use anything at Ark. Strangely, after I'd been working there for a couple of days, Joe Lacossi, one of those in whom I'd confided, told me that Bob had approached him. "You know, I think George is planning something very dangerous," Bob had said. "I think he's planning to climb the World Trade Center. I just hope he's very careful about it." Whether Bob was psychic or someone slipped, I don't know; he never mentioned it to me directly.

It took me three days to machine a prototype. It was constructed of tool steel and aircraft aluminum. My design was for a break-apart device: two pieces, with a strengthening third inserted between them to prevent bending. The device had to be disassembled to be inserted in the channel, then screwed together. This way it could never fall out; it would only slide up or down. The device, which featured a square camming section that fitted inside the channel, had no moving parts.

A couple of days after completing the device, I went to the World Trade Center alone to try it out. It was around 10 P.M. and quite dark. I chose the least visible and most accessible corner, the northwest edge of the north tower, adjacent to the West Side Highway. It's right on West Street, which is deserted at that hour as the office workers have long since gone home. A large sculpture stands directly in front of it.

Kneeling by the building, I installed the device in the channel and tested it. Its action was too stiff; although it could hold my weight, it didn't slide as smoothly or lock as effectively as I would have liked.

MY ORIGINAL DRAWING OF THE FIRST CLIMBING DEVICE. *TOP TO BOTTOM*, A SIDE VIEW, AN OVERHEAD VIEW OF THE DEVICE DISASSEMBLED, AND ASSEMBLED.

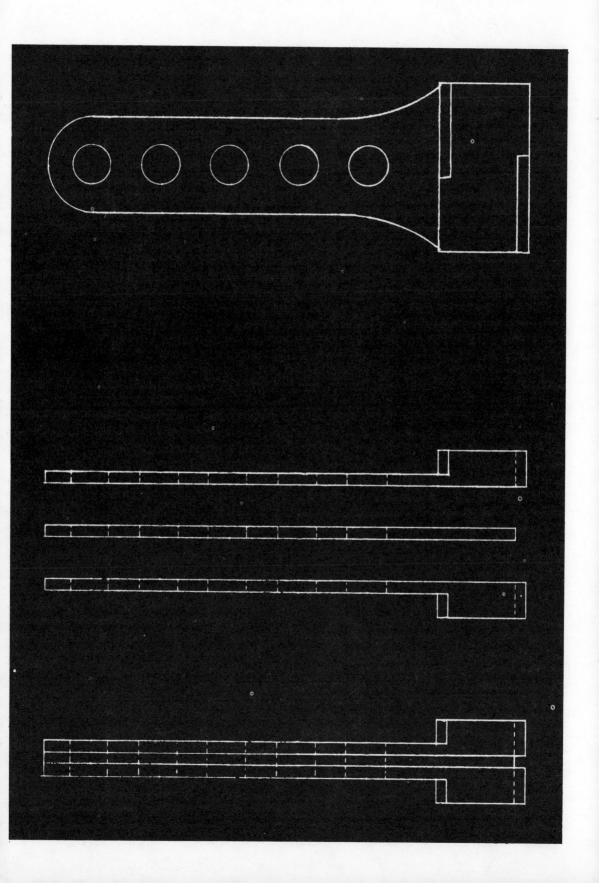

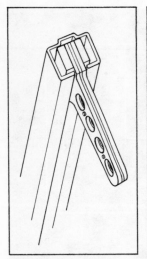

ABOVE,
AN OVERHEAD VIEW
OF THE WAY THE
FULLY ASSEMBLED
DEVICE FITS INTO
THE CHANNEL.

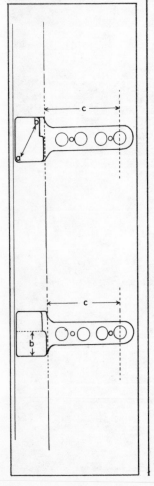

The next day, I was back at work on it. Two kinds of adjustments were required. First, so that it would slide more easily I brought down the overall dimensions of the camming section that would fit inside the channel. Then, to improve the cocking (or locking) action, I cut a slot in the cam; before, the surface had been too long to obtain a secure purchase. A simple problem lies at the heart of this. If the distance between the diagonally opposite contact points (a) and (b)—those portions of the cam that will actually lock against the channel—was very long relative to the length of the lever (c), the device would never cock; it would simply slide down the channel. Conversely, the shorter the distance between these points, relative to the lever, the more positive the locking action would be.

The principle is a very basic one in mechanics, and it lies behind the functioning of this device. What was required of the instrument was to translate a force relative to a distance in order to create friction, which was what would hold me up on the wall. This is how it happens: if you have 150 pounds of weight, and (b) is 3 inches and (c) is 9 inches, then you get three times as much force—(c) relative to (b). Three times 150 pounds pushing against the channel will prevent the 160 pounds (me) from taking a plunge. That's why I had to shorten (b); it was just a matter of leverage.

On the arm of the device—the lever—I'd machined four lightening holes. Depending on which one of these I chose to attach my sling to, I could adjust the amount of force on the channel (by varying, in effect, the length of the lever). I didn't want to put too much strain on the channel, and these holes provided me with a means of finding a happy medium.

The same night, I went back to the World Trade Center to test my adjustments. After installing the device, I attached a sling to it, raised the instrument high in the channel, then jumped up and down on it. Its locking action was fine now, and, as I found when I took my weight off the device, the ease with which it slid in the channel was also much improved. Over the next two months, I machined five duplicates—two each for Jery and myself, and two spares for safety. It was a busy summer; I was in my last term at St. John's, carrying a full load of courses, and had begun ballooning. Tooling is laborious precision work, and each device was extremely time-consuming to produce. I stole away to Ark whenever I could.

In August, as all this was going on, I made my only visit to the observation deck of the World Trade Center before I did the climb. Randy was with me. With a pair of binoculars I surveyed the details of an adjacent corner, checking that the channels went all the way to the top. Just above the channels, in the section of the roof that angles up to the level summit, I noticed there was a small trapdoor; on this occasion it was open. Perhaps it would be a point of exit, I thought. Then I took a number of pictures of the building's design features, and we went down. From a distance of ten or twelve blocks, as Randy and I were walking away, I stopped to look at the towers again. They appeared vast, unapproachable. Leaning against a storefront I tried to count the windows and the floors, dreaming of what it would be like up there. I had a long way to go.

By the end of August, I'd manufactured the six devices and a couple of clamps that could be bolted to the channel. In the event of a problem with one of the climbing instruments or the need for a long rest, I could attach one of these and dangle from my position without fear of falling. Theoretically, I suppose I was ready for the climb from that time on. Physically ready, that is. For now the mental reservations held sway. As long as I was working on those first devices, expending energy toward a specific goal, I'd been fine; but now that this work was done, I was faced with the decision of whether to do the climb or not, and the doubts flooded in. Clearly, I had a lot more thinking to do about the climb; my psychological conditioning was far from complete.

A VIEW OF THE WIN-DOW-WASHING AP-PARATUS AND TWO TRAP DOORS AT THE SUMMIT OF EACH TOWER, TAKEN ON MY RECONNAISSANCE VISIT TO THE OBSER-VATION DECK.

Most important, there was the matter of a backup device; from the beginning, I'd decided that I needed one. While I had confidence in what I'd done, I didn't want to rely on a single system, one design. If any complications developed I wanted to have alternatives. With two types of devices I'd be comfortable. The problem was that although I'd played with a number of designs while I was making copies of the prototype, I hadn't come up yet with anything that satisfied me. My ideas would have worked, but they were all too complicated to make and unwieldy to operate.

After I'd completed the six devices I went back on a night in early September to the World Trade Center with Jery. I wanted to test each of the instruments and to show him how they worked,—and that they *did*-work, in order to build his confidence. West Street was empty when we got down there about 11 P.M. Jery stood lookout while I installed a couple of devices. He said he'd whistle if anyone was coming. I was hunched over the channel bolting a device together when a voice startled me: "Hey, buddy, what are you doing?"

What about that warning whistle? I turned around. Jery was standing off in the distance; he'd been looking the other way. It was a Port Authority policeman.

On his walkie-talkie, he called another cop, who joined him inside a minute. The two of them walked up to me. "What do you think you're doing here?" one demanded.

"Well, I just finished taking out these clamping devices I have," I explained. "I'm an architectural engineering student working on a graduation project. I came up with a design for a safety device for window washers"—my ironclad cover!—"and," I finished breathlessly, "I was testing it here on the building."

"Well," one of the cops answered, "you know, this building

A VIEW FROM A
LEDGE AT THE GUNKS
AT SUNRISE.

has *automatic* window washers. Men don't even go up on the side of the building."

My mind raced. "I know, but there are other buildings that have the same kind of channels"—another fabrication; I had no idea and in fact was wrong—"and, if you remember a few years ago," I rattled on, "a couple of men died when their scaffolding failed and they fell off the Equitable Building and they got killed and I just thought it would be a good idea..."

They mulled this over for a while. "Well, yeah," one of them allowed. "It sounds good." Pressing my advantage, I installed a device in the channel and showed them how it worked. "Look at this," I said as I slid it up the channel. "Here, see?" I said, pulling down on it. "Try this out," I urged them. One of the cops reached up and pulled down on it. The device locked. He turned to the other cop. "Hey, try it." The second one reached up and tugged it, too. "Wow," he said, "it looks good. Good luck with it."

"Thanks," I said.

Briefly, one of the policemen became politely official again. "You know, you should have gotten permission from the building management to do this."

I nodded. "Well, I'm really not doing any damage to the building," I explained, "and I thought they'd be a little hesitant to give me permission to do anything like this, so I figured it's simple enough to walk to the side of the building and try it out myself."

"Well, okay," the cop said. "Good luck with it."

I thanked them again, and Jery and I watched them walk away into the darkness. Then we looked at each other. We were smiling for a long while before we allowed ourselves to laugh.

During the remainder of September, October, and November, I did little toward the climb, apart from thinking, now and again, of alternate devices. A number of possibilities suggested themselves, but there were no brainstorms. So I simply put my devices aside and waited. The weather had turned cooler, and I resolved that I'd do the climb in the early spring. Heaven knows, there were enough things happening at this time to keep me occupied. In late September, I began planning the Unisphere film, and work on it carried me through October. I had begun to see a lot of Randy. I went climbing whenever I could. Often Randy and I would climb at night and sleep on ledges high up the cliff. I love sleeping on ledges. In the morning when you awaken, the view is beautiful; no one else is around; and it's very quiet, like no other place.

Then in November, a call came from my old friend Jim Tinguely at Ark. Two weeks later I was working for Ideal Toy.

THE CORNER AS SEEN
FROM THE GROUND.

THE VIEW TO THE NORTHEAST.

"**W**hat floor are we on?" Glenn and Dewitt were asking the people in the windows. The two of them were bellowing to be heard through the glass, using sign language and exaggeratedly mouthing words. "These windows are *packed*," they reported to me. People were writing the floor numbers on pieces of paper and holding them up. "Sixty-five!" Glenn called out.

"Where is he?" those inside were asking.

"*Here*. Right here!" Dewitt and Glenn would answer, pointing.

"How is he?"

"Great! Fine!" They's make a circle with forefinger and thumb.

"You wouldn't believe all the people in this office looking out!" Dewitt and Glenn were having a ball now. They were flirting playfully with the girls in the offices.

"Man, this one is *nice*," they'd exclaim. "Whoa!" They were cavorting on the scaffolding, ardently spreading their arms, puckering for aerial embraces. "Hey, babyeee! Hoooo!"

I'd climb up a couple of floors, then they'd catch up with me. At every floor people were pressed against the windows, and as Glenn and Dewitt ascended they could peek up the girls' dresses, like naughty boys at a frat party. "Whoooooooooah!" they were squealing. "Ohohohoh!" "You should be over here, George!"

"I'm really missing the views, eh?"

"Yeah, you better believe it!"

Stopping to rest, I removed my pack and took out my water bottle. After I'd taken a sip, I pointed and said: "I live out there in Queens. Right near those big buildings." The Little Neck, North Shore Towers complex rose up in the distance, across the river. We were all pointing out sights we recognized.

"It looks like Bear Mountain up there," Dewitt said, turning toward the Hudson.

"There's Coney Island," Glenn observed, pointing east, where the Atlantic lay shimmering in the sun. Closer, the city had opened up beneath me as I climbed higher. The Woolworth Building—until 1930, at sixty stories the tallest building in the world—with its handsome Gothic spires, tiers, parapets, and gargoyles (the "Cathedral of Commerce," it was called), stood just a couple of blocks to the north. City Hall and a stately white cluster of municipal buildings lay beside it, and a bit farther east, huddled low to the ground, I could pick out the colorful pagodas and banners dotting the narrow streets of Chinatown.

I was even in height with the high core of midtown, and the southern half of Manhattan stretched between those buildings and me like a valley. Occasionally an airplane would lazily pass above, seeming hardly higher than I was as it circled around the tip of the island over the lower bay in its approach to La Guardia or Newark. People were gathered on the tops of adjacent skyscrapers, incongruous figures beside the great,

MIDTOWN MANHAT-
TAN SEEN FROM THE
WORLD TRADE CEN-
TER.

impersonal hulks of the air-conditioning machinery on the roofs.

As I climbed again, the three of us talked. They told me about their jobs. Dewitt often worked at heights on rescues. "But this is something else!" he said, meaning the exposure. Glenn had once wanted to be a city cop too, but when he saw there were no openings he'd settled for the Port Authority. I told them about the Gunks and about climbing, why I did it, how I savored the excitement. Neither of them had ever tried it, although Dewitt has a brother-in-law who climbs. "The guy loves it. He goes all the time," he said, which sounded familiar. Dewitt said he might like to give it a shot some day. Glenn had his doubts; he was a little afraid of heights, he admitted. We all laughed: he was nearly seventy stories up on a thin scaffolding in a stiff breeze. Fine place for him to be!

Considering Glenn's lack of experience in this sort of mission—Dewitt did this kind of thing all the time—he was perhaps an odd choice for the assignment. I'd later learn his pairing with Dewitt, whom he'd never met before that morning, was the curious result of a jurisdictional tiff that had erupted between city police authorities. The Port Authority Police had claimed me as their responsibility, inasmuch as the Port Authority owned the building. They'd send *their* guys down on the scaffolding, they insisted. Yeah, but this is New York City, the N.Y.P.D. countered, which is *our* responsibility, so we should send one of our guys down. Eventually a compromise was reached in this impromptu summitry, and each authority agreed to send one representative. It is perhaps fortunate the scaffolding was no larger.

At the seventy-fifth floor, Glenn said, "Hey, why don't you give us your autograph?"

"Really?" I asked them.

"Yeah," they said, "you're gonna be famous. C'mon, give us your autograph."

"All right," I laughed. I stopped climbing. Dewitt and I leaned over toward each other, and he handed me a pad and pen.

I thought for a moment, then wrote: "Best wishes to my co-ascenders, from the seventy-fifth floor." I scribbled one for each of them, added their names and the date, and signed them. Then I passed them along and started climbing again.

Hammering a device, pushing it along the channel, stepping up. Thirty-five stories to go.

In early November when I finished work on the Unisphere film, it was time to take stock: I had a degree in environmental studies, a little savings left, which wouldn't last long, and no idea about what I was going to do next. How, for instance, was I going to earn a living? While the notion of doing something in film appealed to me, that seemed about as practical as my liberal arts degree. Chance in the form of Jim Tinguely's unexpected call stepped in again nicely and, for a while at least, put my uncertainty to rest.

Jim and I had become very close in our years together at Ark. Over long lunches and coffee breaks, we'd talk about philosophy, stalk the big imponderables, roll our curiosity around the latest of Erich Fromm, exchange books to read. We talked easily and often and had much in common. A few months before, Jim had moved to California, very briefly as it turned out. He and his wife had given away or sold almost all their possessions, loaded what was left in a van, and headed west with their kids. What Jim found when he got there was a culture that seemed youth fixated, play oriented, and materialistic; almost everyone he met was divorced. Disgusted, he repacked the van and drove his family back east. Now he was working for Ideal Toy. Unaware he had returned, I was very pleased to hear from him again.

Jim was setting up a model shop at Ideal, and there was an opening for another model maker. Would I be interested in having a look at the place? Over lunch one day, he filled me in. Until his arrival, no one in the Think Tank (the department responsible for conceiving and developing most of the company's toys) had been specifically assigned to build models. As a result, toy inventors either had to go outside the department to get their ideas executed or mock them up themselves; few inventors had the experience and none the proper equipment. The shop was a shambles.

It made sense to have model makers on the spot. Inventors' ideas could be built sooner and more professionally, and, as a result, they would stand a stronger chance of finding their way on the market. What Ideal needed was an inventor who was used to working in three dimensions; someone who could take charge of the shop and specialize in model construction. Jim had been hired to expand the Think Tank's operations along these lines.

Despite my lack of clear alternatives, the idea of reentering the nine-to-five world didn't transport me. Still, working with toys sounded like fun, all the more so if it meant working with Jim again. And when after an interview (for which I did my first-and-only resume, typed by my mother the night before), Julie Cooper, vice president of research and development, offered me a job, I decided to give it a try.

As it happened, I loved the work. I'd been hired primarily as a model maker, for which my background at Ark was perfect training. In the shop, there were lathes, milling machines, table and band saws, belt and disk sanders, drill presses — components of a world in which I felt entirely comfortable.

Yet I was also expected to function as an inventor, and this was an area in which I had less confidence. How did one go about inventing a toy, or anything else for that matter?

I needn't have worried; the atmosphere of the Think Tank was remarkably stimulating. People batted around ideas all day long, and I was surprised at how often I'd find toy ideas surfacing. It was certainly very different from sitting alone at home and trying to think up a toy. (Most people have a greater capacity for invention than they suppose. Since working at Ideal I've become convinced that almost everyone has a million-dollar idea in the course of a lifetime, but few are in a position to act on it or even perhaps to recognize it. The Think Tank supplied that context.)

Ideal is a giant, pulsing factory, filled with injection-molding machines and other manufacturing equipment. Tucked away in a corner of one warehouse on the fourth floor is a plain door identified only as "517." Behind this door is the Think Tank, where most of Ideal's toy ideas originate. It is a large room with many glass cubicles arranged in an L-shape around an inner chamber, the shop. Tools lay everywhere (and probably still do); the room was a jumble of pieces of plastic and metal. There were parts of dismantled toys, whole toys, and toys in every stage of completion. Littering the tables and floor and desks and drawing boards (each of us had one), were toys that would never go beyond this room and toys that would be bought by the millions.

Many at Ideal didn't even know where the Think Tank was. Out of the 600 or 700 people who worked for the company, no more than 30 or 40 knew what was going on in 517. Executives at Ideal went to some lengths to preserve this secrecy. It was a little like working at the Pentagon. Except, of course, that here we were building toys (and not war toys, either).

To get into the building, an identification card with picture was required. Escorts accompanied all visitors. Entry to various areas of the factory was restricted; passes, issued in different colors, identified one's level of access. Only inventors and top executives enjoyed unlimited entree. The door to the Think Tank was locked at all times, and inventors — who, with senior executives, alone had keys — were quite strict about who gained entry. The only person in the sculpture shop (which took care of the likenesses and cosmetics on the models) who had access to 517 was its boss. Janitors were required to clean the room during the day, when inventors were there. Those in the Think Tank were thus invested with a certain mystique, and it was assumed (inaccurately) that one of the trappings that went along with it was money. This was an idea inventors, enjoying the aura if not the actuality of wealth, did little to dispel. People

MY IDEAL I.D.

JIM TINGUELY AT
MILLING MACHINE.

also assumed that the elite inventors, whom they imagined playing with toys all day, had all the fun. They were right.

There were about fifteen of us in 517, and we were freed from paperwork and other intrusive drudgery. As model makers, Jim and I had more day-to-day deadline pressure than the others, who had only to juggle two questions: what would make a good toy and how would it work best? Each inventor had his special strength: some were particularly good commercial artists; some specialized in electronics—the hottest new thing in toys; some were mechanically inclined; and others were gifted in strategy and game concepts. People in the Think Tank tended to have a seat-of-the-pants knowledge about things; few had much education or formal technical training. The person most adept at electronics, for example, picked it up soldering breadboards. Work in the Think Tank was largely intuitive, and these inventors' specialties were really mostly knacks—but knacks carried to a high level of sophistication, to the point where they'd lead with some regularity to patentable inventions.

The one thing everybody shared was a sense of creativity and spontaneous thinking. Aside from that, the place was a bin of colorful eccentrics.

Our senior member, at perhaps sixty, was Frank Vincent. (This name and those of others in the Think Tank that follow have been changed, but the details are accurate.) Frank was (and is) an inveterate tinkerer, given to whipping together all kinds of oddments: a radio aerial might be soldered to a spoon and—eureka!—a spoon with a telescoping handle would appear (Frank called it his "boardinghouse spoon"). Beside his desk he kept a cabinet of toys whose major theme was erotic. A typical item featured two lovers on a bed; wind it up, and the man and woman would frenetically swive away. Frank used to make all his own models, never even bothering with preliminary drawings—he was so clever he didn't have to. He was also tumultuously insecure. If any of his ideas met with resistance, he'd more erupt than react. "Goddammit!" he'd shriek. "Why did I put all this time into it? You don't know a good toy when you see one!" Company executives took great pains to gentle him. "Frank, you're great," they'd answer. "You're really doing a good job." In fact, he was. When it came to toys, Frank was brilliant, extraordinarily prolific. A day didn't pass without his coming up with a new toy idea.

Another inventor, Claude Wolfe, was a raffish figure in his mid-fifties and a captivating raconteur. He had a home in West Virginia, where his soon-to-be ex-wife and children lived, but he holed up in a small apartment in Jamaica, Queens. Claude was given to squiring opera singers around town and, in fact, there was something operatic about Claude, too. A Princeton graduate and enthusiastic avocational painter, he specialized in games. Claude had had a remarkably varied career; he'd been president of his own toy company, which he'd lost, as well as art director at a number of ad agencies. Sometimes several of us would sit in his office for half the day, wonderfully entertained as he spun stories about his escapades. Claude has since moved to England and remarried.

The fellow in the office next to the one Jim and I shared was a funny and very likable engineer named William Randall. An excellent draftsman, he was particularly good at figuring out the nuts and bolts of how ideas might be made to work. William lived (and still does) with a woman, but he was always calling up other ones. "Hey, baby," we'd hear him crooning in his deep, deep voice, "what do you say we get together tonight and . . . who *knows* what'll happen?" Then: "Okay, okay. Maybe I'll give you a call in a couple of weeks." William was always on the make; he called it "dealing."

A bit farther away from our office was a cubicle with an oscilloscope and a maze of wires, burrowed somewhere amidst which Ed Wenders, an impressively resourceful electronics expert, could usually be found. The strangest noises would emanate from his office: baby cries and sirens, high-pitched whoops and weird ullulations. Ed was another one given to inventing odd gadgets. Once I came on him sitting with his eyes closed, one hand tightly grasping a cylinder that made a humming noise gradually climbing higher and higher in pitch. "What're you doing, Ed?" I finally asked. He'd invented an item, he told me, that would measure how active a perspirer you were; the more your palm sweated, the higher the sound would climb.

Near Ed sat Roshi, an Indian who was so quiet and low-key that sometimes we wondered if he was there at all, surrounded as he was by a jungle of mango trees, tropical plants, and seedlings being nurtured. At night, Roshi would leave on his desk lamp for the plants. Occasionally I'd stop by and we'd talk about horticulture. All around Roshi were the hand tools he insisted on using, clinging to an older way of working that he found comfortable. Roshi's special field was games. Although technically he was a model maker, too, one rarely thought of him that way; the idea of throwing something together was utterly inconsistent with his personality. Deadlines didn't exist for him. But there was a real need in the department for the kind of work Roshi did. Particularly adept at delicate sculpting, he made beautifully detailed, precision models. His meticulousness and patience were a real reserve.

The presence of another inventor, Phil Fontaine, was as insistent as Roshi's was inconspicuous. Phil had the habit of twisting others' ideas around to make them sound like his own. In the Think Tank, bull sessions would begin with almost anything, usually work their way around to women, and at last might even touch on toys. Often a good idea would emerge from these sessions. If one did, likely as not Phil would offer a slight modification, triumphantly exclaim "I got it!" and run into his office to begin sketching. Soon he'd take his design to Julie Cooper and exult, "Look at this idea I had." As you might expect, Phil wasn't the most popular person in 517. The thing was, though, he was smart. All the people in the Think Tank were there for a good reason.

Henry Shorell, another talented inventor, always thought he was on the verge of losing his job. Henry's problem was that although he used to come up with excellent ideas, often involving sophisticated electronics (radio-controlled cars, a skeet-shooting set projected on a wall), they were often prohibitively expensive to produce. Remarkably often, this didn't prevent them from being marketed. Because Henry was an absolute terrier. He'd fight furiously to get his ideas accepted. Ideal executives would repeatedly say no to him, *absolutely no, Henry, now forget it*, but Henry would come at them again and again and again, each time changing his design ever so slightly, wearing them down until finally they'd throw up their arms and he'd have another toy in production. He was an odd mix of aggressive confidence and insecurity. To stave off the firing that he considered imminent, Henry was always working.

It's hard to say just what constituted satisfactory productivity in 517. "Give us one a year," Ideal executives used to say. In a business where a single toy can generate many millions of dollars in sales, one successful toy a year would, not surprisingly, have been considered quite satisfactory. So would a couple of moderately successful inventions. Some inventors whose ideas had worked for the company in the past might go several years between inventions without having to worry about their jobs. A model maker might have invented no toys at all, but if he'd helped others to develop theirs, his contribution was considered significant. For reasons that will become clear, it was very difficult to get a toy idea accepted for production. Many excellent ideas, some of the best ones in fact, would remain just that. It is a very subjective business.

We used to play with toys and games for hours on end. Practically daily, someone would haul out his latest invention, and we'd all try it, talk about it, offer suggestions.

Usually, however, this kind of public airing came after an idea was fairly well along. For the net of secrecy surrounding Department 517 extended within it as well. Until they'd developed a notion, inventors were generally circumspect about what they were working on, lest someone else (especially Phil) appropriate it. Each of us usually had one or two others we'd use as a sounding board. Even (or sometimes especially) when your ideas were undistinguished, it was easy to fall in love with them; so it was essential to have someone whose opinion you valued and whom you could trust.

Jim and I worked on a number of secret projects together. One of the best, Jim's idea initially, was a set of dogfighting airplanes. Circling a pylon, they passed each other above and below. Each player had a joy stick. Pull back on it, and the plane would accelerate and ascend; push down, and the plane would drop. The object of the game was for one of the planes to chase the other and knock it down. Then it would plummet to the ground and crash. It was a fantastic idea, like a road-racing set with the added ingredient of altitude and all the more fun for it.

The invention caused great excitement in the company. Everyone with access to the Think Tank, from the president on down, kept coming in to play with it; we had to install new batteries every few hours. Julie Cooper said it was the best toy he had ever seen. Jim and I felt the same way.

Then sadly (and perhaps inevitably given the way Ideal worked), the idea started to slip away from us as others began imagining kinks. First, the engineering department, responsible for estimating a unit price, said it would cost a lot of money to produce. That much we might have predicted. Costing is a tricky process (how much would it cost to produce each piece? how many hours would go into the assembly process? how much would the box and graphics cost?), and engineers have been known to estimate high to protect themselves, often reducing the chances of a good toy being produced. (Relations were understandably strained between the practical engineers and the flighty "creative" types in 517, who would occasionally discover that their careful designs had been altered for the sake of efficiency.) In this case, the engineers were wrong. Jim and I knew the toy wouldn't be expensive, and after many estimates engineering finally came around to our way of thinking.

But now Ideal executives wanted to give the toy a more "current" theme. Jim had used biplanes for the aircraft. Given the *Star Wars* rage, however, they decided that space was the thing. Battling spaceships, it was thought, would be just right. It was ludicrous: they took an ingenious little toy and transformed it into spaceships going around in circles. This cashing in on a fad is typical of toy manufacturers, but it would only have ended up dating the toy; when the space craze ended, so would the hunger for the item. Eventually, for reasons known only to themselves, Ideal executives decided not to produce the toy at all. (Today, several years later, the word at Ideal is that company officials are once again considering manufacturing it. With biplanes.)

Most of my work was on mechanical toys. For example, someone might have a concept for a doll that kicked, and my task would be to concoct a mechanism to make it do this well and cheaply. The challenge in toy design is always to devise a toy that works, is as inexpensive as possible, and is durable (of the three, durability is usually the first to go). Plastic toys provide an example of how difficult this task can be. They're made by injection molding, in which molasseslike plastic is poured into a cavity, then cooled. Although it sounds easy enough, there are many things to consider. What is the simplest, most efficient tooling that will produce a piece? How and where will the two halves of the mold come together? How thick should the plastic be? You can't make a section *too* thick; the thicker it is, the longer it takes to cool (meaning fewer can be produced), the more it shrinks, and the more sink marks result. To avoid this (and effect economies), ribs are used rather than solid sections, and cavities are placed wherever strength isn't needed. All of these are integral elements in a toy's design. The greatest idea will never be realized unless a simple, economical way to produce it is devised.

To familiarize myself with how basic problems in toy design had been approached in the past, during less hectic periods I enjoyed visiting the stockroom, where parts left over from toys no longer in production were stored. I'd raid these supplies for the use of the Think Tank. Then, in sectional boxes, I'd catalogue my discoveries: motors, gears, metal strips, different-shaped pieces of plastic, and various sizes of wheels. This way, the components of old toys became the basis for new ones.

Then, too, if I saw a toy on the market that interested me, I'd buy it, disassemble it, and study it. Ideal would reimburse me for the purchase. This was common practice among the inventors.

Another source of ideas was right in our department, where there were large ceiling-high shelves full of all kinds of toys— old and new Ideal products and those of other manufacturers. Once in a while, I'd climb a ladder and browse through them. Perhaps I'd take several apart, if I was curious about how they worked. Other toys could provide you with a vocabulary of mechanics. Occasionally, when I needed a given piece for a model, I'd remember how it had been used in another toy and where I might find it. This was similar to the way in which I eventually developed the design for my second climbing device. I adapted a common rope-climbing instrument—not the mechanism, but the idea behind it.

One big project on which I worked at Ideal is a particularly good illustration of the relationship between cost and simplicity and of how important a knowledge of past solutions to problems in toy design can be. This was the development of a toy film projector with sound. Another company had begun work on the project, then gone down the tube; Ideal hired an inventor, Ira Cavrell, who'd worked on it there. These were the givens: the film was perforated in the center (so that it was really a 4 mm format on 8 mm film), and it would wind on a reel (as on an eight-track cassette). Basic problems remained to be solved, however, and chief among them was the shutter arrangement. I was assigned to work on the project with Ira.

His idea was to use a prismatic cube, synchronized with the film, as a shutter; it would blink the light on and off so that the

AT MY DESK AT IDEAL.

lines between the frames of film wouldn't show. Light would be transmitted only when the faces of the cube were perpendicular to the beam. As soon as the cube turned and the sides shifted, the beam would be reflected away. This would have been impractically complicated and expensive to produce.

PROJECTOR.

Then Ideal hired a new engineer whose idea was to use something called a Geneva Drive Assembly, a sophisticated, high-precision device that rotates a shaft a quarter-turn at variable intervals. I thought both men were bonkers to be speculating in these terms for a toy. So while I was trying to make their ideas work, I was developing my own solution.

It was no startling innovation. I merely adapted what I knew had been successfully employed in other toy projectors. My arrangement was simplicity itself: as the film wound, it jumped on and off a registration pin next to the gate. The pin would halt the film and pressure would build up behind it, causing the frame to jump quickly ahead. Then the next perforation would catch and the process would be repeated. All this happened very rapidly. What it accomplished was speeding up the movement of the film from frame to frame, so that the dark areas in between went by so swiftly as to be invisible. The shutter had just one moving part, the film going by. It was really the only economical solution, and for this reason was adopted. While the others would have worked well, they would have made the so-called toy nearly as expensive as an adult projector, which was silly.

While the Think Tank was expected to be the main source of toy ideas, it wasn't the only one. Sometimes people in other departments or company executives had ideas that would come to us for further development. Sometimes the company bought, either outright or on a royalty basis, the ideas of outside inventors and companies. In an average year, perhaps a quarter of all the items marketed originated outside the company.

For a time, Ideal kept on a retainer the Jack Ryan Group, a kind of independent think tank headed by the inventor who created the Barbie doll and was later (briefly) married to Zsa Zsa Gabor. (More units of the Barbie doll have been sold worldwide than all other dolls combined; what made the doll so special was that it had tits, the first doll to feature them. Reinventing breasts made Ryan a millionaire; Zsa Zsa was perhaps a more predictable step than at first glance.) Ideal paid Ryan a hefty retainer each month to supply ideas for toys in development. Ryan's group devised, for example, a silent motor energized by yanking a string for a doll that Jim invented. Instead of the conventional arrangement in which small lobes rubbing against plastic function as a clutch to keep the motor running slow, the group ingeniously employed a viscous silicone substance that had the same effect.

Unfortunately for them, the Ryan group also worked on the

toy projector. By this time, Julie Cooper wanted to prove Department 517 capable of surpassing Ryan and sought to use the projector as a test case. One day, Ryan and his group, and the four of us in the Think Tank who'd worked on the projector, presented our respective models to Ideal's president. It was a showdown.

Ryan's version, on which his team had labored two years, was very sophisticated, with a complicated shutter and hand-tooled precision parts. It incorporated some revolutionary ideas. For example, the soundtrack was on a record; when the image on the screen was static the projector could freeze-frame and the sound would continue, meaning less film was needed. Their projector had, however, one insurmountable problem: it wasn't a toy.

Ours, the result of only two months' work, was made almost entirely of plastic and had few moving parts. Cheap, in other words; simple, practical, less likely to break. Its soundtrack was on the film—conventional but inexpensive.

Ryan and his staff appeared acutely uncomfortable at this meeting. His people tried to extol the advantages of their model, but it was a losing battle. Those of ours were clear. Shortly after this meeting, the Ryan group was taken off retainer.

Ideal is among the five or six largest toy manufacturers in the world. The company owns related enterprises—Crown Sporting Goods, for one—and an outfit that makes large vinyl toys like kiddy pools. But its most sizable corporate component is Ideal itself, which has a number of divisions: plastic toys (the largest), games, dolls, and preschool. In 517, we worked in all four areas; whenever a line needed filling out we'd concentrate our efforts on it for whatever time was needed.

Interestingly, the company got its start with the original Teddy bear. Inspired by a newspaper cartoon showing President Theodore Roosevelt with a bear cub, Morris Michtom, owner of a small stationary store in Brooklyn, suggested his wife make a stuffed bear. Michtom then wrote to President Roosevelt asking his permission to use the name "Teddy Bear." "I doubt if my name will mean much in the bear business, but you may use it if you wish," he answered. The bear found as large a place in the toy market as it did in the language, of course, and Ideal was on its way.

Later, Ideal made the Shirley Temple doll, which is reissued periodically to this day. It produced Mr. Machine, a vast seller whose innards—which allow him to move forward, swing his arms and legs, open and close his mouth, and whistle "This Old Man"—may be seen through a transparent plastic frame. It produced Total Control Racing, in which the cars can change lanes, and the still-popular Mighty Mo and Mini Mo trucks, which have friction motors geared down—so that the trucks will go for a long while at a realistic scale speed. (Someone,

TEDDY BEAR.

somewhere, is a millionaire because of the idea of gearing down a friction motor.) Ideal produces Tuesday Taylor, a high-fashion doll introduced some years ago to compete with Barbie. The real gold in such an item lies in the accessories. Take Tuesday's convertible chalet-beach house, for example; you flip the roof, winter turns to summer, the chalet becomes a bungalow by the shore, and the doll is ready to be dressed in a full range of seasonal clothes — all manufactured, of course, by Ideal. Not surprisingly, people in 517 are always trying to dream up new accessories.

EVEL KNIEVEL.

Another large seller for Ideal was the Evel Knievel toy. A motorcycle with Evel astride the saddle was mounted on a winder, powered by a crank. As soon as you stopped winding, the cycle would take off; a gyroscope kept it on two wheels. The toy was extremely sturdy — you could arrange nice crack-ups against walls — and had terrific "play value." (By this I mean the ways in which a child, using imagination, can extend the interest of the toy; how long, in other words, he can play with it before becoming bored. A big box, for instance, has a lot of play value; it can be used as a house or a tent; you can enter it and make believe it's a train; you can cut windows so that it becomes a ship or a plane or a car or, for that matter, a bunker. Often the box a toy comes in has more play value than the toy itself.) With Evel and his bike, for example, you could make a ramp using a piece of cardboard and a few books and have him jump in the air. Or set up banked turns. The toy had all the attributes of a motorized car with the added fascination of balance and possibility of altitude. For a while, it was a fabulous seller. Unfortunately, when Evel fell on hard times, so did the toy, and finally it was dropped.

A business that is so highly dependent on the rapidly changing whims of the marketplace is an edgy, volatile one. Although in one year a single successful toy can account for 40 million dollars in business, eventually the market will become saturated; tastes change quickly, and unless the company has another blockbuster to replace it, the company may be in trouble. Booming in one year, large toy companies can be out of business the next.

To minimize risk, most manufacturers stick to areas in which they think they do best. Ideal is known for dolls and plastic toys, but for some reason its executives believe they can't sell board games; if an inventor develops a strong concept for one, they'll transform it to a three-dimensional game, with ramps and the like. Some companies specialize in licensing, buying the right to use someone's name as the peg for a toy — the John Travolta or Cher doll. Others, like Creative Playthings, specialize in preschool toys. Parker Brothers and Milton Bradley concentrate on board games. Mattel does almost everything. And one company exists on Scrabble alone (that's all it needs).

Whatever their products, the annual big event for toy

manufacturers is Toy Fair, a two-week-long trade show that happens in New York just after Christmas. At this time, manufacturers present their lines to dealers, who place orders for the following Christmas season, the prime period for toy sales. The shows at the fair are highly theatrical, like those in the fashion industry (to which the toy business bears a more than casual resemblance). During these two weeks, a company's fortunes either soar or plummet.

Most manufacturers, wary of shelling out production funds for a toy without sizable orders on hand, won't produce their molds until after the fair. Toys displayed are simply models. If trade reaction to them is tepid, they'll progress no further.

One result of this is secrecy. Credentials are required to get into each company's exhibit; only dealers who are potential customers mingle among companies. This happens (or rather doesn't happen) for a solid reason: since most toys aren't in production, it would be all too easy for one manufacturer to borrow the ideas of another, with certain perfunctory modifications. A toy seen in the display of company A during the first week of Toy Fair might appear, slightly altered and for a lower price, during the second week in the arsenal of company B, which would begin taking orders on its wily appropriation. This had occurred more than once. Defending copyright is an expensive and protracted process, so as a practical matter what it comes down to in the toy business is getting a jump on another manufacturer.

Since perhaps half the line at Ideal would change yearly, work was hectic, verging on frantic, before the fair, with people rushing to complete models. Then afterward, things would settle down again in the Think Tank, and we'd begin dreaming of toys that might hit the market in a year and a half to two years.

My dream as an inventor was to build a small electric helicopter powered by a rotor that would fly freely, untethered. A ring of wires, wider than the rotor, would protect the blades as the chopper whirred here and there. If the ring came in contact with a wall or other object it would simply glance off, and the chopper would gently change direction. The problem was the power. Helicopters must be light and the motor and batteries required for such a toy would be so heavy as to make flight impossible. At least for the present. One day a small rechargeable battery capable of generating enough power will be developed, and a great toy will result.

I mention this because what all of us were doing in 517 was playing with ideas, which *incidentally* might become toys for kids. My helicopter, Ed's sweat indicator, Henry's electronic marvels, Jim's battling biplanes—these were all thought up because they were things that we'd have liked to play with ourselves. We were our own best audience. What I thought would appeal to a kid was what would appeal to me.

When I told people what I did for a living it almost always got a big reaction. Usually a mix of lively interest—I was still in a world of toys and the imaginative conjuring they stimulate that most, had left behind—and bemused incredulity, as if there was something incongruous about an adult spending his days thinking of toys and games.

Is there? As people "grow up," many seem to fall into structured niches of behavior, adopting approved conventions. What's often lost in the transition is a sense of play, the kind common to children that seems important to me, a basic part of the enjoyment and appreciation of life.

When I was at St. John's, I remember another student asking me what I planned to do on the approaching weekend. It was midwinter, there'd been a fresh snowfall, and I said I was going sledding. Would he like to come along? "Nah," he replied, "I'm too old for that." Too old? He was maybe eighteen; I was twenty-five.

At eighteen I was still playing hide-and-seek, staging mammoth battles with toy soldiers with my brothers. Battalions would be deployed all over the house. Rubber bands became bullets; the soldiers—they came in three classic poses, standing, kneeling, or lying, always holding a gun—would be propped up against blankets artfully folded as camouflage mountains and supports so that they could sustain a direct hit without falling.

I've never really *stopped* playing. So making, inventing, playing with toys for a living required no particular adjustment for me. It seemed natural from the first. When I went to work at Ideal late in the autumn of 1976, I was so enthralled by it and so busy that I gave little thought to climbing the World Trade Center. Every so often I'd take out my plans for a secondary device and evaluate where I stood. I'd consider other ways I could get to the top, sketching my ideas, then set the project aside again. But in December, as I eased into the rhythm of my job at Ideal, the idea of the climb began to surface again. At this point, I went to work on a backup device in earnest.

"Are you gonna make a movie?" Glenn was asking me. I laughed in disbelief. "I don't believe you guys. I'm just climbing this building. I don't know what you're talking about." The higher I climbed, the more precious the experience of the ascent itself seemed and the less it mattered what happened at the end. I refused to think about it.

Certain that I'd never be there again, I was trying to hold onto these minutes before they became memories. I wanted them to last forever. Several times I stopped and pressed my cheek and palms against the cold steel of the building. I wanted to feel it now, while I could. The building seemed animate, with a force all its own. Pressed against its surface, I felt in intimate contact with it. I was trying to make mental snapshots, to impress on my mind everything that I could feel and see around me, hoping that it would seem real to me when I tried to remember it. I wanted to have it with me always. This was not the kind of experience, I knew, that was likely to come again. It was a time of uncomplicated glory. I was enjoying every second, filled with delight at what I'd done, and filled, too, with wonder at the excitement of it and at the beauty that was everywhere around me.

Down below, everything had taken on the toylike unreality of views from airplanes. Now, at about 9:30 A.M., the streets around the World Trade Center were still packed with spectators. People on the tops of nearby skyscrapers were taking photographs and waving, and for the first time my ebullience brimmed over and I waved back happily. On some rooftops there were just a few people, on others large clusters.

Every so often, Dewitt would report in to his sergeant. "All right, we're at the eighty-fifth floor now. Things are going okay."

"You getting tired?" he kept asking me.

"No, I'm fine," I'd reassure him. "I'm all right."

Although Glenn and Dewitt were good high-spirited company, I couldn't help wishing they weren't there. The climb had become another thing with them. I wanted to enjoy it alone, as I had started it. I missed the uniqueness of the absolute solitude. A few times I was on the point of asking them to take the scaffolding up to the top so I could finish the climb alone, but I didn't. They had a job to do; they were considerate; they weren't interfering; I didn't want to rock the boat.

As I approached the top I spoke less to them. They were still fooling around with the people in the offices and between themselves. As we ascended, they kept track of our progress. "What floor are we on?" Glenn boomed into an office at one point. Someone held up a sign. "Oh," Glenn said, "ninety-one."

I climbed up to the next floor. The scaffolding followed.

"What floor are we on now?" Glenn called through another window.

"Ninety-two," Dewitt answered dryly.

"Right. Of course!" Glenn burbled in embarrassment. "And that floor was ninety-one. That's why I'm a Port Authority cop and you're with the city." We all laughed.

I was nineteen stories from the top.

MY VIEW.

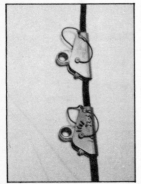

JUMARS.

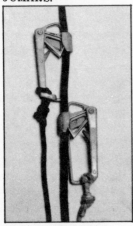

GIBBS ASCENDERS.

MY ORIGINAL DRAW-
ING FOR THE SECOND
CLIMBING DEVICE. *A*.
SIDE VIEW OF THE
HOUSING, CAM AND
LEVER. *B*. SIDE VIEW
OF THE PLATE THAT
FITS INSIDE THE
CHANNEL, AND *C*.
BACK VIEW OF THIS
PLATE. *D*. TOP VIEW,
THE CAM. *E*. FRONT
VIEW, THE HOUSING.
F. TOP VIEW, THE
HOUSING. *G*. TOP
VIEW, THE WAY THE
HOUSING AND PLATE
FIT INTO THE CHAN-
NEL WHEN ASSEM-
BLED.

Early in December, I moved from my parents' house into my first apartment on my own; I can recall setting at my drawing board there studying Gibbs Ascenders and Jumar Ascenders, mechanical rope-climbing devices (of the type I'd use more than a year—and dozen worlds—later in my climb for ABC of Angel's Landing in Utah). The Jumar features a spring-loaded cam that locks on the rope; the Gibbs, on the other hand, has a cam that pivots like a seesaw—a climber's weight on one end of the cam rotates the other end so that it clamps on the rope. This latter type became the model for the device I was planning.

Looking at the Gibbs, I studied the formation of the cam's curves and the angle at which they gripped the rope. An important thing distinguished the way it worked from the kind of thing I'd need. A rope, especially a climbing rope, is compressible. For this reason, the Gibbs cam had teeth and traveled over a long arc—across the distance through which a rope could pass and then still farther as it squeezed against the rope itself. Since my device would have to bite on steel, however, it wouldn't need teeth and the distance the cam had to travel could be shorter—just wide enough so that it would engage against the channel and then retract enough to no longer be in contact with it. To achieve this, I simply offset the cam's center so that the whole thing was, in effect, closer to the surface against which it would lock.

After sketching a number of different ideas for adaptations, I finally hit on one that pleased me: the device would have a plate that would fit inside the channel and then be bolted to the outer housing. Like a Gibbs Ascender, the instrument would have only one moving part, a cam. From the *outside*, the cam would jam against the channel, pinching it against the inner plate. Pretty much empirically, I figured out the probable dimensions of the device, then completed a set of working drawings (distinguished from sketches in that they're precisely composed with drafting tools and include dimensions).

Next, I showed them to William, the engineer who occupied the office next to mine at Ideal. Although I didn't say what I was up to, I tolh him how I wanted the instrument to work, showed him a drawing of the channel in which it would fit, and said how much weight it would have to support; my life might depend on its reliability, I added casually. Right away, William smelled a rat. "Is this something you're using for ballooning?" he asked.

"No, no," I said.

"Oh, I know," he guessed next. "You're probably going to climb the Empire State Building or something like that."

"Naw," I said. "I'll let you know what it is, but I can't tell you right now. It's on the Q.T.," I explained. (I actually use expressions like that.)

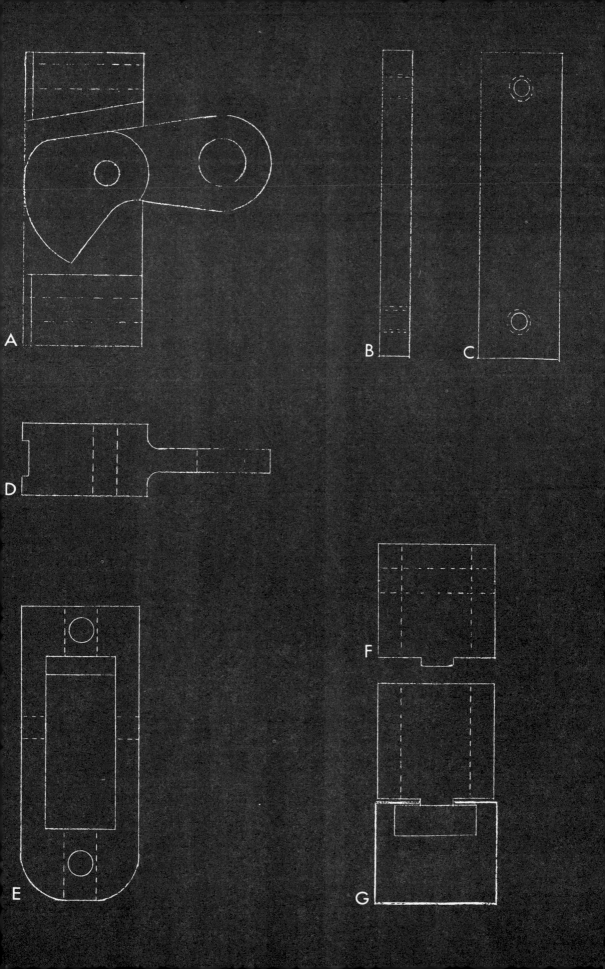

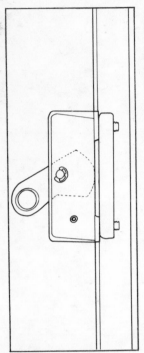

THE DEVICE, ASSEMBLED IN THE CHANNEL, IN LOCKED POSITION.

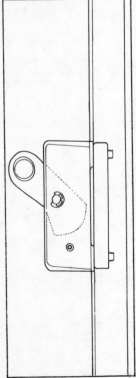

THE DEVICE IN UNLOCKED POSITION.

"All right," William said, and we did some calculations. We computed whether the strengths I'd provided for the materials would be sufficient and, a little more basic, whether the device would work at all. Initially, William was skeptical about the design, then after a few days of figuring at home, he was *sure* it wouldn't work. He decided the coefficient of friction between the stainless steel of the channel and the cam I'd designed was inadequate to keep it from sliding.

On paper, he was doubtless right. Still, a scientist, I knew, can sit at a drawing board and work with figures all day long, but until an idea gets a practical test, he really knows very little about it. This is, of course, a key problem in research. (Later, after the climb, William took me aside. "Hey, listen," he said. "Don't tell anybody that I said it wouldn't work." Then he wagged his finger at me. "I knew you were up to something like that.")

And so, despite William's reservations, I went ahead and began constructing a prototype; this was in late January. For materials I chose tool steel for the lever or cam (which I later had oil-hardened because it would receive the most wear), unhardened tool steel for the plate that would fit inside the channel, and aircraft aluminum for the housing. Oil-hardened tool steel is phenomenally strong, but at maximum stress it will snap or crack rather than bend; since I had no idea of the oddball stresses the climb would involve, I thought some backup system advisable. To that end, I added a simple safety mechanism to the housing: a 900-pound-strength loop of cable to which I'd be attached. This way, if the hardened-steel lever somehow broke and I started sluicing down the channel, the friction of my weight pulling the cam against the track would be enough to arrest any fall.

It took me about a week, working at Ideal, to manufacture the prototype. In early February I took it down to the World Trade Center for a test. Although the device didn't fit properly in the channel, I saw the adjustments would be minimal: several small cuts in the housing and cam to bring them down a little in size. A couple of nights later I was back at the base of the tower. Now the instrument worked even better than I'd hoped. Its locking action was absolutely secure and its motion through the channel smooth. It worked so well, in fact, that I decided to make it the primary device and relegate my first design to a backup position.

Over the next two months I built five more of these devices. Work ended at five-thirty at Ideal; in spates of four or five days I'd stay until nine-thirty or ten at night, hunched over the milling machine. I spent most lunch hours the same way, when I wasn't making side trips for aluminum or tool steel or strength bolts. The work was terribly time-consuming. Tool steel, even unhardened, is very firm; only five or ten thousandths of an inch can be cut away at a time. Moreover, since I was working on such a precise scale, I had to jig up

special tooling (custom-made clamps) to hold the metal so that
it could be mounted and maneuvered over minute distances on
the milling machine. To make it all still slower going, it was
necessary to reassemble this tooling and break it down each
time I worked.

Why had I become so obsessive about it now? Certainly in
midwinter there was no hurry. Yet since the day in
Washington Square Park, whether or not I was actively
thinking of the climb, my excitement had been steadily
building. Now its accumulated force had taken over and was
driving me on. During this time, as I was actively working
again toward making the climb happen, my mood soared
higher and higher. I was running on an adrenaline high; it was
the longest sustained period of exhilaration I've ever
experienced. Often, as I worked, I trembled with excitement,
sometimes with fear. Projecting forward, I'd imagine myself
on the side of the building. The sound of the milling machine
seemed far removed from the use to which its products would
be put; yet that sound was bringing me closer and closer, and I
knew it.

Back in the early summer, when I first began thinking of the
climb, it kept spilling over into conversation, the way anything
would that was at the front of your thoughts. I probably
mentioned it to fifteen people. Even once to a complete
stranger, a photographer whom I met in Battery Park during
the celebration of Op Sail on July 4th. (I'd gone alone, unable to
find anyone not intimidated by expected crowds; my friends'
mistake—it was a day of rare, and shared, high spirits.) But
now, apart from bringing Jery up to date occasionally, I spoke
little about my plan. From time to time I might tell Randy
what I was doing, or mention it to Jim at work, but there was
only so much to say about it and I didn't want to bore them; it
was *my* project. At this time all my concentration was going
into the production of the devices.

In March while I was still working on them, Jery told me
he'd changed his mind about coming. The more the devices
developed, the more imminent the climb seemed to him, I
suppose, and the more seriously he began to weight his
decision. Back in June it had only been a distant plan; now,
gradually, a fun idea had begun to grow intimidatingly
concrete. He realized that it was actually going to happen and
probably soon.

It wasn't the idea of the climb itself that worried Jery. Rock
climbing, we'd trusted each other with our lives many times
before. He had confidence in my ability to work out a device,
that would minimize the risk and insure our safety.

Rather, it was his concern about the climb's repercussions—
the legal trouble he feared would follow. In fact, Jery felt so
strongly about it that he tried to talk me out of doing it, too.
This would be the third stunt on the building, the third strike.
This time, he argued, the authorities' patience would be at an

end. They would want to make an example of me.

Jery's doubts seemed extreme to me, but that month I did a little research on what *had* happened to the two fellows who'd used the World Trade Center as a stage. Randy and I had driven up to the Gunks on a weekend that had turned cold; she didn't feel like climbing, so instead we went to the New Paltz Library, where I looked up Philippe Petit and Owen Quinn in the *Reader's Guide to Periodical Literature*. For his aerial peccadillo, Philippe had been charged with reckless endangerment, criminal trespass, and disorderly conduct. He'd strolled on a one-inch cable strung between the tops of the two towers, he said, because he wanted to put on a show (a performance that, with all his equipment and a reconnaissance via helicopter, had cost him $12,000). His sentence showed a nice sense of congruency with—as well as an appreciation for—his original intentions: he had to put on a free show for children in Central Park. Case closed.

Owen Quinn's stunt—he parachuted off the top of one of the towers—was another matter. His jump, which very nearly cost him his life, was a kind of plummeting editorial. He did it, he stated, to call attention to himself and to the plight of all the starving children in the world. With its frantic careless brevity and off-center rhetoric, his gesture lacked the winning breathtaking whimsy of Petit's. After being charged as Petit had been, Quinn was sent to Bellevue for observation, then released. A year and numerous court appearances later, those charges were finally dropped. (No one requested he parachute into Central Park.) What did this tell me? Perhaps patience *was* ebbing; perhaps it wasn't. In any case, it was simply another unknown and I wasn't going to let it stand in my way.

Soon after Jery let me know about his decision, I asked my brother Steve to take his place, but he turned me down, too. His wedding date was set for the late spring, a time when he preferred not to be in prison. Next came Sam Moses, a climbing acquaintance who worked for *Sports Illustrated*. Early in the fall of 1976 I'd mentioned my plan to Sam and to Peter Rossi (my bridge-playing companion from the Gunks) as we were walking along the East River near Sam's apartment. Sam was quite interested and asked to go with me. We might become famous, I recall him saying. I suggested we go down to the buildings and take a look. Standing at the base of the corner where I'd been testing my devices, I showed them the channel and explained how the devices worked. At this point, Jery was going with me, I told Sam, but if for some reason he dropped out we'd talk about it again. The idea of Sam as a partner had made me a bit uneasy; he'd had only limited experience in climbing. I wasn't certain how comfortable he'd be at extreme heights. In the spring, when I told him about Jery's decision, I discovered that Sam had come to share my reservations. It was, he decided, too ambitious for him.

Then I tried Peter Rossi, who also declined the invitation.

Peter worked for a large New York bank and thought it an act
unlikely to boost his image there. Finally, I asked Randy, who
immediately said yes. But after mulling it over for a while I
decided that I didn't want her to do it after all. If anyone was
going to come with me, I wanted it to be because my
companion's enthusiasm for the climb was every bit as
compelling as my own. That way, there'd be no way I'd feel
responsible if anything went amiss. I knew the devices inside
out (having designed and built them), knew what I was doing,
and — because of my climbing experience — knew how to take
care of myself if problems arose. But if someone else had
trouble — if, for example, he or she were suddenly to become
frozen with fear or a device were to malfunction — that person
might not be quite as resourceful about it as I trusted myself to
be. Randy, I knew, would have been doing the climb for *me*,
and important as her gesture was to me, it wasn't a reason for
which I wanted her to take that kind of risk.

After Randy, there was really no one else with whom I
wanted to share the experience of the climb. I concluded that
the most reasonable thing was to do it alone. Which, of course,
made it all the more scary. There was a big difference between
planning the climb alone and *doing* it alone. Circumstances,
however, shaped the event rather differently from what I'd
intended. As it happened, doing all the preparation for the
climb alone, as I had been, was probably the best possible
conditioning for the emotional adjustment I had to make.

I'm getting ahead of myself. At the end of March, when I had
almost finished the last of the devices, I made another visit to
the World Trade Center. By this time I'd made perhaps ten
trips there, almost always at night. Occasionally, I went to
show a friend or two how the devices worked. Sometimes I
went alone, just to assure myself that they *did* work. Only once,
back in the fall, did I install two of the devices; installing and
then disassembling them consumed too much nervous-making
time. Ten feet was the highest I ever climbed; I never had an
impulse to go higher. Had I been caught, it would have been
necessary to keep climbing — this would have been my only
chance — and I wasn't nearly ready. The climb was something
I wanted to be the culmination of a carefully coordinated effort,
not of a moment's carelessness. On this occasion in March, I
slipped a device in the channel, tested it, and left quickly.

As March ended, it was getting down to the wire. I had the
first set of six devices and now the second set as well. I had the
little metal clamps I could bolt onto the channel in case I had
any trouble. I had several other prototypes, in varying stages of
completion, for other less successful ideas that I'd discarded
along the way. Just a few things remained to be done on my
primary devices, but now I put them aside again, kept them in
my drawer at work, and waited. It was still quite cold. I'd do
the climb, I decided, when it was warmer, when I had the

devices finished, when I was *ready*. I didn't want to rush it. I didn't want to be rash. I wanted my psychological preparation to be as thorough as my mechanical one.

Around this time I was also getting very self-analytical. Is this how people kill themselves? I'd wonder. Is this how they push themselves over the edge? What is it in me that makes me want to do this thing? Am I *crazy*? Is this how sanity steals away, while you seem sensible to yourself—perhaps *only* to yourself—all the while? Lying in bed at night, I'd look up at the ceiling trying to picture what the climb would be like, what would happen. I had no idea at all, and the uncertainty frightened me. A nagging suspicion persisted that I'd missed something, perhaps something crucial. On my way down—for sometimes as I lay there, I imagined myself falling—would I be saying to myself, Man, I never thought *that* would happen? Would I berate myself then for not considering this critical element—whatever it was? It was all an unknown, and I was hard pressed to anticipate the contingencies.

Maybe I never *will* really climb it, I began thinking. Why did I have to put myself in that position? Why did I even have to contemplate it? I didn't have to go up on the side of that building. Try as I might to bury the climb, however, it kept coming back; I was for it, against it, almost as if I were riding a manic depressive swing.

At such moments, I'd try to bargain with the part of me that was unrelenting. I've made the devices, my mind would run, and I've done all the planning. I can *always* make the decision to do it, even twenty years from now. Why did I have to do it so soon? Why did I have to force myself into thinking that I had to do it right away? Accompanying this conservatism was a chorus of other fears. Would people think I was a screwball? Would they laugh at me? What kind of changes might it bring into my life?

Certainly the realization that it might get publicity occurred to me, albeit never on the scale of what happened. A story on the local evening news, perhaps; a few articles in the paper. Anything larger seemed a possibility, never a likelihood. At one point, for example, kindled by my recent experience on the Unisphere, I considered trying to find someone to film it. But then my skepticism would take over again. How ridiculous, I'd think. Who would be interested? Besides, the logistics of such an undertaking were overly complicated, and the filming would detract from the spontaneity of the climb. It would become an event calculated for the cameras rather than for myself. (For this same reason I chose not to bring a camera myself; any interruption of the experience seemed a violation. I didn't want to confuse the climb with anything else. I didn't want taking pictures to get in the way—in any way.) While possible implications occurred to me—and led me to this kind of thinking—I found it necessary to dismiss them. It seemed likely to me that my act would be greeted more with consternation than with ovation and that people would regard me as a nut rather than a hero.

And so, through late March, April, and early May, as the weather warmed, I stalled and waited. I still hadn't completed the devices, though just a few hours' work remained to be done. The plates that would fit inside the channel needed to be drilled out and threaded where the bolts would come through from the main body of the device. I had to install the axles on which the cams would swivel. When I finished this work, however, it would be time to make the climb. Which was precisely why I was avoiding it. I wanted, *needed*, to keep the excuse of not having completed the devices.

There was still another element in my delay, although this in itself would never have checked me. I hoped that the World Trade Center authorities would open the plaza, which had been closed for construction since the previous summer. For reasons discussed earlier, I wanted to do the climb on the northeast corner of the south tower, but a large fence encircled the construction now, obstructing my path to it. I was afraid that if I tried to scale the fence I'd be seen and halted before I reached the building.

That particular corner held another attraction for me that I haven't mentioned, which is in turn connected to the climb's appeal to me in the first place. Had I merely wished to do the ascent as a feat—that is, to see that it could be done and that I could do it—I might have climbed the building at night, when the chances of being apprehended were so much less. But my motivations weren't quite this simple. In fact, I had three reasons for doing the climb during the day—two obvious ones and a third that was a little more involved. The first was that I wanted the view, and as I've said, a particular corner afforded the best one. Second, I wanted a few pictures of the climb and—this is a measure of my naivete about the reaction the ascent would produce—would later ask a photographer friend to record it from the plaza.

The third reason was connected to the first: if one corner offered the best view of the city, then the inverse was also true—it was the corner that could be *seen* best from the city. This was not a negligible attraction. Being noticed, becoming an outlaw, had a definite appeal. I savored anticipating the sight that would greet the dense columns of workers thronging their way into office buildings: a single man high on the stark, impassive wall of that tower where no one was ever meant to be. I relished the climb's renegade extravagance; it was brash, and that aspect of it held a powerful allure for me. Up to that time it was not a side of me that I had much indulged, but it was nonetheless part of my makeup and now it was demanding to be noticed.

For years, I'd gotten a kick out of people's reactions to things I did—the white-water tubing and the ballooning and the climbing. I didn't need it—these were things I would have done anyway—yet I enjoyed it. And at the same time, I found it odd that so many people were impressed. Why didn't *they* do these things, I'd wonder? These pastimes seemed so available and natural to me. So much lies waiting out there beyond the regular workaday world; there is absolutely no reason why life should be boring. And though I'd laugh when anyone considered me an adventurer, the image pleased me all the same and I can't entirely dismiss its effect. The idea of being unconventional still appealed to me.

So while fame and publicity didn't matter to me, the outrageousness of the climb certainly did. Up to this time, the only thing remotely like it that I'd done was the Unisphere film; that three snips could get permission to do something so unusual enchanted me. Initially, of course, the climb (and the film before it) had merely seemed like fun things to do. It was only when I asked myself what others would think that the acts appeared outlandish and all the more attractive for it. The idea of a crowd increased the magnitude of the event, added to the adventure. If I was going to do this thing, better that it be before a multitude than a single sleepy guard.

SPECTATORS NEAR
THE WORLD TRADE
CENTER.

Five stories from the top, I was climbing slowly, trying to hold onto these last moments. Because of the shapes of the windows and facade of the opposite World Trade Center tower, I was unable to see the crowds watching from within; the windows are narrow, and the white columns protrude at an angle that creates a jumble of reflections. On the top of the other tower, however, I was able to see the craned heads of observers peering down over the edge. And above me, the catwalk from which the scaffolding was lowered was crowded with watchers. At the top of the corner I was climbing, I could see a hand extending a mirror; someone afraid to look over the edge had devised this method of less queasy-making viewing. I relished it.

A VIEW FROM THE
TOP.

By mid-May, my excuses for delay had begun to seem boring. The early-April date I'd set during the winter for the climb had come and gone by more than a month. It was time, I told myself, to fish or cut bait. To face up to the climb and do it, or decide now, unequivocally, to drop the whole thing. I knew that I'd have a lower opinion of myself if I continued to put it off.

And yet I also knew that I'd invested too much time and emotional energy in the climb *not* to do it. My efforts had come to a head, and I was getting itchy. It was like that moment on many ascents when you are on a thin exposed ledge and facing a still more frightening crux; you can retreat in fear or move forward to go beyond it. You can do anything, in fact, but stand still.

Something happening at Ideal then made me even more impatient to move forward. Every couple of weeks we used to have brainstorming meetings in the Think Tank. At one of these sessions, Phil came up with an idea that nearly unhinged me. This was for a figure concept—a doll for boys, in effect—called the Invisible Man. Ideal's president thought the idea was an inspiration. The figure was to be clear plastic, with (in one plan) opaque liquid within. At a signal, perhaps the push of a button, the liquid would drain out, leaving the clear plastic head and clothed figure—so much for invisibility. Imagination was to have made up the difference, and, who knows? perhaps kids would have loved it. But I thought it was idiotic. Jim and I were delegated to make it work.

At first, I resigned myself to the project. What did I know? If these people were so hepped up about it, maybe it would sell. Phil began making sketches and bought a number of kits for the Visible Man (a figure whose arteries, organs, and other innards are visible) by the Renwald Company; we planned to adapt this basic design. My task was to construct the torso for the model. From the start, the idea was a nightmare to execute.

How would the opaque liquid drain, for example? I tried building a bladder or reservoir that would hold it. In one version, when you pushed in on this bladder, the liquid would go up into the head; then if you turned the figure upside down, the fluid would remain in the head; if you did it again, it would drain back into the torso. All the volume from the head, however, wouldn't fit into a single reservoir below, and so it was necessary to put reservoirs in the legs. Then we couldn't get all the liquid from these reservoirs to go back up into the head.

Jim worked on another idea that involved using air. In this scheme there were two balloons—actually prophylactics, the only thing that had the necessary degree of stretch—one in the head and one in the torso. Pressing the one in the torso would deflate it and inflate the other one, causing the head, the theory went, to gain or lose visibility. Unfortunately, what it looked like more than anything else was prophylactics deflating and inflating.

We'd sit for hours staring at these silly models, cursing the idea, grinding our teeth, hoping to hear that the project had been canceled. Jim called the figure Scum Bag Man and Dickhead; he'd hold it above a wastebasket and drop it in, announcing, *"In-Visible Man!"* We *hated* it. This was in mid-May, and it was really the final thing that motivated me to do the climb. You can just climb out of this project, I began to think. At the end, scaling the World Trade Center came down to an escape from . . . the Invisible Man.

At the same time as this was going on, I was also moving into a new apartment in Hollis, Queens, tediously shuttling all my things over in many little trips in my VW Squareback. Between the move and work, I was bored, restless for some excitement.

Still another element urged me to do it now. At the back of my mind was the other group that I'd heard, back in the fall, was planning an attempt. The pioneer aspect of the climb was a strong pull; I wanted to be first. That others wanted it, too, made it a more valuable prize. If I was going to lose it, I didn't want it to be for waiting.

And so all the factors were converging. The weather was beautiful. Everything indicated it was time. Now I began remaining after work at Ideal to put the finishing touches on my devices.

Even so, second thoughts nagged at me. My brother Stephen's wedding would take place in a couple of weeks, and I didn't want to miss it. Ideal would probably fire me, I remarked to Jim as we talked over what the consequences of the climb might be. He thought it unlikely; in fact, it was his guess that company executives would be delighted by the climb. Still, it was certainly a possibility, he acknowledged, and not one that pleased me much.

Finally, abruptly, one Saturday I decided to do the climb during the following week. Arbitrarily, I set Wednesday as the date. I'd come to depend on my excuses too much, I realized. They had to stop. Now they did.

Taking so many months had served an important function in minimizing the anxiety I felt. Accepting the full commitment of actually scheduling a date was the last stage of the decision-making process, the sign that my year-long psychological conditioning to the task was at an end.

On the same weekend that I settled on a date, I announced, during a family barbecue at the home of my sister Terry and her husband, Richie Carberry, what I planned to do. It was no great surprise to my parents, I suspect. They'd had a notion I was plotting something; perhaps one of my brothers, Paul or Steve, both of whom had known about the climb from the start, had let something slip. Now I made it official. Considering what I was saying, the reaction was remarkably casual. No dramatic silence greeted my statement. Other conversations continued as I spoke. Addressing Terry and Richie with my parents listening, I said that I was going to climb the World Trade Center soon, probably that week. I'd been planning it for a while, I added. To do it, I'd made special mechanical clamping devices that I intended to use on a corner. It was something that I was very excited about.

That this produced no particular response amazes some people—one friend told me that if he'd made that announcement his parents would have had him committed—but it was just what I expected. Although my brother-in-law told me my mother appeared a bit unsettled by it, her agitation was slight enough for me not to notice. My father was characteristically blase. Nobody tried to talk me out of it. No one asked why I was doing it. My parents were *used* to my exploits. I went climbing all the time. They knew I did this kind of thing. For the same reason, the plan surprised none of my friends.

This was also the occasion I chose to tell my youngest brother, Frank, about the climb. Waiting this long certainly wasn't for lack of feeling or trust between us. But it was a difficult period for Frank, who was shy at the time, in need of bolstering. He'd dropped out of high school in his sophomore year. Our age spread is so great—twelve years—that I've always felt protective of him. On the one hand, I didn't want to dazzle him with my ambitious schemes; if I could avoid it, I didn't want him to think he was competing with me. On the other hand, I didn't want him to have faith in me doing the climb, and then, if I chose not to, let him down. For these reasons, it seemed best to say nothing almost until the last. After this night, everyone in my immediate family knew.

One more cause for delay presented itself the next day, Monday, when I remembered that a month earlier I'd promised to give blood this week—on Wednesday. At first, I thought I'd skip the donation this once. But then I felt bad about it; since I'd said I would do it, I thought I should. So I decided to postpone the climb one last time, by one day. Anyway, Randy, who was a schoolteacher then, had a field day on Wednesday, and this way she'd be able to see the ascent (or so I thought). It was possible, of course, that giving blood might sap my strength at a time when I most needed it, but all such considerations, everything that was permitting me to duck the climb, had grown tiresome and I decided to ignore it as a factor.

This wasn't all that easy. Even under the best of circumstances, I find giving blood rocky going: that big needle in your arm, the bag slowly filling, the thought of all that rich blood coming out of *you*. To make matters worse, because my blood-sugar count is a bit low I pass out easily when I do it. Six months before, during Ideal's last blood drive, I hadn't been permitted to be a donor for this reason (not because giving was harmful to me; what the program administrators were afraid of was that people would see me swoon and bolt for the door). This time, I didn't mention my problem. When my turn came, I simply told the nurse that since giving blood made me a little dizzy I liked to have my legs raised and to lie there for a while afterward. When I was one pint lighter, I lay on the cot for a good twenty minutes, taking no chances. Then, feeling fine, I went back upstairs to the Think Tank, telephoned Julie Cooper's secretary, Eleanor Lopez, and informed her that I was taking the next day off, as a personal business day. After hanging up, I took Jim aside and told him: this was it. I was very elated.

Jim was the only one I told at Ideal, and I let very few people outside the company know: Jery, who'd be driving me down to the building; Randy; Ron Di Giovanni; Mike Cardacino, who'd be taking pictures; and my family. I wanted to be autonomous in my decision making.

During the past months, telling people about my scheme hadn't made me feel any responsibility for going through with it—the idea was so offbeat that I could always have said I'd decided it was crazy. But a specific date was something else. If, for any reason, I chose not to do it that day, I didn't want the pressure of a crowd of people waiting. And so when I told anyone my plan, I was intentionally hazy about the timing; maybe in a year, I'd say. Curiously, no one in whom I confided asked me when (or whether) I was actually going to do it.

After work on Wednesday, I went home and gathered my things together. For a couple of weeks, I'd had my equipment spread out on the floor of my apartment, where I kept looking at it trying to decide if I'd chosen the right things to take. Every so often I'd substitute a piece of gear, or eliminate or add one. That evening, feeling both determined and committed, and also rather strange—for after all these months it was finally going to happen—I put my things in my pack and went over to my parents' house. It was a mild evening, just starting to darken. By coincidence, my brother Paul and his wife, Greta, were there when I arrived. We all sat down together in the living room.

"Well," I said, "I'm going to climb the World Trade Center tomorrow." I took my instruments out. "These are the devices I've made," I said, and showed them how they worked. I reassured my parents that the devices worked well and safely, that I had backup equipment, that I had tested it all out a number of times. As a result of what I was going to do, I expected to get into some trouble, I said, but I wasn't sure how much. Probably I'd have to go to Bellevue Hospital. Even so, I hoped to make Stephen's wedding, set for that Saturday.

"It's all worth it to me," I told them. "I didn't ask for permission because I knew it would be denied. I'm better off just going out and doing it. I know it isn't really considered to be legal. I just want to do it so badly I can't help it. I've wanted to do it for months. I *have* to do it."

A long silence. "You're almost twenty--eight years old," my father said. "What are we going to do, tell you that you can't do it? You can make your own decisions." Both my parents looked at me steadily. "Are you *asking* for our permission?" my mother said.

"No," I said. "I just thought you should know."

"Well, God bless you. God be with you," my mother said simply.

It was an emotional moment. My parents were very serious now, no longer casual, and so was I. While I didn't think I was going to die—I wasn't being morbid about it—the thought occurred to me, and probably to them, that we might never see each other again. At no time now did I think of the changes the climb would introduce into my life, of how different everything might be when I saw them again. That evening, anticipation of what the next morning held for me was so overwhelming that I was scarcely aware of anything else.

My next stop that night was the World Trade Center. To reduce the chances of being intercepted the next morning, I wanted to install the plates and bolts of the devices in the channel; this way, it would only take me a few minutes to get set up and be on my way. Feeling the need of company then and eager for lookouts, I asked Paul and Greta to come with me. Paul was tired and had other plans, but Greta drove down to the towers with me. Apart from a few scattered tourists, the area was deserted. Strolling hand-in-hand around the plaza, looking at the sights, we pretended (without ardor) to be lovers.

All the while, I was making certain there were no security guards around. When I felt sure, I knelt at the corner of the building and, as Greta kept watch, quickly installed the parts. One last look at the tower, rising sleek and white in the darkness, and we left. After dropping Greta off in Queens— she had me wait while she went inside and got me a piece of steak for my breakfast—I drove home. It was around eleven o'clock when I got there. Before I went to bed, I set my alarm for four-thirty.

At the top of the corner I was climbing—as is true of each of the towers' walls and corners—a ten-foot-high, sixty-degree incline angles up to the roof. Those inclines and the flat roofs to which they lead sit like caps atop the towers. Just above where the channels end on the corners, and on this incline, are two small doors, each perhaps two feet wide by three feet high. My plan for getting off the climb, once I'd reached the top of the corner, was to work one of these trapdoors open and crawl into it. That failing, I figured I could throw a rope with a skyhook attached over the edge of the roof, where it would catch; then I'd pull myself up. In any case, I wasn't worried. By that time, I knew I'd be at ease on the building; I'd figure something out. It was, after all, only a matter of moving up ten feet at the top. My devices would still be in the channel; if I slipped, they were strong enough to stop any fall.

Now these trapdoors were open. Three floors from the summit, I took off my pack. "Here," I said to Dewitt and Glenn, "I won't be able to fit in that door with this thing on. Would you take it up for me?" Stretching to my right, I carefully handed it to Dewitt. My shoulders had been aching; it was a relief to have it off.

One story later, a cop's head popped out the trapdoor. "How you doing?" he asked.

"Fine," I said.

"Feel okay?"

"Yeah."

"Listen," he said. "I'm gonna lower a rope down to you. It's got a hook on the end. I want you to hook it to yourself."

"No thanks."

He lowered the rope anyway.

"No. No thanks. I don't want it," I said. "Not yet. I'm really fine. I'm perfectly safe. I've gotten this high without it; I'm over a hundred floors up. I'll be okay," I reassured him.

"No, take the rope."

The line still dangled there beside me. I looked at it. "I wish you'd just take it up," I said, very politely. He pulled it in.

"Hey, we're going to go on up now," Dewitt said. He and Glenn congratulated me. "See you later, huh?"

"Thanks for sharing the experience with me," I said to them. "It was nice." We smiled at each other warmly, then they rose to the top on the scaffolding.

Climbing again, I worked my way up until I was only five or six feet from the trapdoor. The cop was leaning out slightly—*very* slightly. With perhaps a 5000-pound test line he was anchored to a beam, part of the superstructure of the building. It was a rig that might have supported a Chevy. He lowered the rope and hook again.

"*Please* take this," he urged me. "Just clip it on. We don't want to lose you now."

I laughed. "I'm really not gonna go anywhere."

"Clip it on now," he said. "C'mon, take it."

"All right," I said. "If it'll make you happy I'll clip it on my harness. But don't pull on it."

At this point Dewitt and Glenn were talking to the people at the top.

"All right," the cop said. "When you get up here, just stick your head in and we'll pull you in headfirst."

"No, you won't," I said. "I'm getting up on my own way. I want to go in feetfirst." I wanted to finish the climb in style, as I would have if no one had been there. The policeman did not look happy.

"Don't worry," I said. "I feel very safe here. I'm used to heights. I know what I'm doing. I think it'll work much better if I just go in my way, the way I'm comfortable. I'll go in feetfirst."

When I reached the top he was holding the rope so that it was taut between us.

"Don't *pull* me like that," I told him. "I can't move around. You're making it very hard for me to move."

The line remained taut. So I leaned backward away from the building, pulling on the rope and, incidentally, pulling him farther out the trapdoor into my world. As we had this little tug-of-war over who would be boss, I could feel him trembling through the line. He was very nervous. At this moment I'm sure he felt responsible for my life. And, perhaps, a little anxious for his own as well. "Don't pull on it," I insisted.

He relaxed the rope very slightly. Right up near the edge now, I gave a short wave, one motion of my hand, to the people on the summit of the other tower. It was a large crowd, I could see now, of reporters and camera crews filming away.

Then, using the same short motion, I waved to the crowd below. A tumultuous cheer rose up to me, a mix of horns and roaring voices, as if the city were a vast stadium that was erupting in glee. It was a giant, reverberating *whoosh*, like the repercussing echo of an explosion. The volume of the crowds, even at that height, astounded me. It was unbelievably loud. I felt embarrassed by it; it seemed too much. What had begun as a very personal, private experience had turned into this, touched so many. It was hard to connect the two.

Now, to pull myself up, I grabbed onto an angled metal beam behind the trapdoor.

"Don't pull on that! That's weak!" the cop exclaimed. It was probably only holding up the building.

"What do you mean, it's weak?" I said. "It's been here for a couple of years. I'm not that heavy. I'm not gonna pull it down." In any case, I was still attached to my devices.

"Don't pull on it!" he screamed.

I wasn't going to argue. Reaching farther back, I found a larger beam. He was really very nervous. "Don't worry," I comforted him. "Really, I know what I'm doing."

"Take it easy now. Take it easy," he was telling me at the

same time, gentling me as if I were a skittish colt.

Where the top of the corner meets the incline to the roof, there is a two-inch lip, on which I was perched. As I started to stand up, I found that my waist strap, still attached to one of the devices, was restricting me. With no slack in the line, I couldn't go up any higher "Wait a minute," I said, and knelt back down to unclip the waist strap. Then I stood up again. Holding onto the beam, I swung my feet in.

The cop was still trying to pull me in.

"It's okay. Okay. I can get in all right."

Feetfirst, I shimmied in. Then I turned, leaned out, slid my devices up and out of the channel, and gave one last short wave to the crowd below. It was 10:05 A.M. They were still cheering.

ENTERING THE TRAP DOOR.

AFTERWORD

At eleven o'clock the next morning I was standing beside Mayor Abraham Beame at a mobbed City Hall news conference. Spirits were high; as I entered, flanked by the Mayor and Police Commissioner Michael Codd, the crowd of reporters, unabashedly partial, whooped and whistled and clapped. It was hardly the conclusion I expected, but then the past day had been packed with surprises.

After the climb police had arrested me in the nicest, most congratulatory way possible, and charged me with reckless endangerment, criminal trespass, disorderly conduct, and unauthorized climbing of a building. The city had in turn sued me, through the unamused office of the Corporation Counsel, for $250,000, its supposed cost in attending to the fuss. (Commissioner Codd would shortly scale this estimate down to $2500). The reaction of the public was a different story.

Crowds had followed me through the streets of New York, hailing me happily wherever I went. In the past twenty-four hours, my ascent had been featured on the front pages of newspapers across the country and of scores more abroad, as well as on the local and network television news. I had appeared on NBC's Today program and ABC's Good Morning America (both of which had covered the climb as it was happening the previous morning), in addition to several local television news and talk shows. Already, commercial offers had begun to pour in. It seemed likely to me that I'd climbed not to the top of a building, but to another planet.

Now the Mayor, quick to turn an embarassing miscalculation in which he'd played no part into a public relations bonanza, was declaring that the city was dropping the lawsuit. Instead of $250,000, we were settling out of court for $1.10, a penny a floor, he announced, drawing applause and laughter. (A real bargain—it costs $1.80 to take an elevator to the World Trade Center's observation deck.) In return for this, I had agreed to discourage others, likely to be less well prepared and less experienced than I, from following suit. I had also, the Mayor revealed, suggested a design change that might frustrate future attempts on the towers' walls to William Ronan, Chairman of the Port Authority. (Of course a resourceful and persistent climber will always find a way of doing things). Several weeks later, after I'd promised no repeat performances, the criminal charges against me were also dropped, as this press conference pretty much assured they would be.

A happy ending in other words, and a long way from Bellevue or a jail cell. (One postscript: it developed that my climbing devices, which Fire Department officials initially thought could be adapted for rescue work, had no applications beyond the one for which they were designed; the World Trade Center towers are the only buildings with that type of channel.) Things would not be the same for me again, however. The morning of the climb I'd been another face in the crowd; a day later I was that special creation of the media, an instant international celebrity. The enormous, sudden changes that the climb introduced into my life can't be crowded into the final chapter of this book. But I'd like to give a general idea of what followed, and make a few observations along the way.

Almost from the moment I stepped off the climb I was deluged with offers for movies, books, promotions, television appearances, lecture tours, other climbs, endorsements, television ads, and charitable appearances. In the eyes of many, I became a potential publicity machine, a walking dollar sign, a commodity to be packaged; there was capital to be made, and scores of entrepreneurs were chafing to help me make—and share—it. No one could have been less prepared to deal with this than I was. "I'm a babe in the woods," I told a reporter at the time, and I was hardly exaggerating. I didn't know what to do.

My first move was to take a leave of absence from Ideal. I needed time to sort it out, respond to requests for interviews, and get some advice. "Strike while the iron is hot, kid," people kept telling me, pressing their business cards in my hand. "It's a once in a lifetime chance." "Take the money and run."

Instead, for a long while, I simply ran. To date, I've probably turned down several hundred thousand dollars worth of offers. Most of them caused me little hesitation. Promoters asked me to climb the Sears building in Chicago (the world's tallest), the Transamerica building in San Francisco, the John Hancock Center in Boston, and a newly opening shopping center in Connecticut (I was offered $25,000 for this one alone). A Texas entrepreneur wanted me to climb an oil tower, a Hawaiian television show tried to induce me to climb Diamond Head, and an Australian radio station wanted me to scale a tower, which they'd specially construct. A New York savings bank tried to recruit me for a television ad in which I'd pose in front of the World Trade Center. A "talent packager" suggested sneaker endorsements, or perhaps an ad for razor blades; surely I'd be willing to shave my beard? Still another promoter proposed a televised "grudge match"; wasn't there some other well-known climber, Sir Edmond Hillary, say, with whom I had (or could develop) a rivalry that we could settle in a tv competition? And so on.

It wasn't that I was averse to making money, or taking advantage of some of the opportunities that were being offered. But my climb of the World Trade Center had clearly meant something very special to a lot of people. And if they found inspiration in my taking up a dramatic challenge for its own sake, then I considered it my responsibility to leave that inspiration intact. At no cost would I taint the image of the climb with tasteless commercialism. I certainly wasn't going to become a carnival act.

Some people, of course, would remain convinced that I did it for the money and attention, that it was all a cagey, if daring, self-promotion, another hustle. "What's your angle?" one television reporter asked me repeatedly. "I have no angle," I told him. People still say to me, "Well, you've got what you wanted, haven't you?" I answer, "I always *had* what I wanted." I never wanted or valued celebrity, never equated money with happiness. I'd always lived very simply and privately, and wanted to keep it that way. In any case it would have taken a psychic to predict the reaction to the climb. (No, I didn't consult one.)

Yet hype is everywhere around us, and people are deeply—and often reasonably—suspicious. Still this can reach ridiculous heights. Dozens of people have asked me, for example, if I didn't fall on purpose during a 1978 ascent, televised live by ABC, of Angel's Landing in Utah's Zion National Park. Consider it: I was twelve hundred feet up on a sheer wall, anchored to the crumbling sandstone by just one tenuous nut. Maybe people think that anyone crazy enough to be up there in the first place will do anything. But to suppose that I valued my life so little that I'd *purposefully* plunge thirty-five feet and career off the wall—risking a much longer fall—all for the sake of boosting the drama is downright silly. It indicates how deeply rooted our expectations of show-biz manipulation are.

Sometimes, reading or hearing reactions to my World Trade Center climb, I've felt the surprise and fascination a writer must feel when readers draw meanings from his narrative of which he was unaware and that he never intended. To me, scaling the World Trade Center had the same kind of meaning as any other challenging ascent. The delight I felt afterwards was only different in degree, since so much had gone into the climb. To others, however, I've learned that it had different, larger meanings. It pleases me that in a time of depressingly passive diversions (like television and other drugs—I'd much prefer that someone go hiking rather than watch *me* on television) the climb might serve as an example to young people of how much the world can be enjoyed with a little imagination; that in seeing me achieve a goal that appeared impossible (except to a practiced eye), people might have found a renewed or heightened sense of what we're all capable of.

If I could choose any meaning for people to draw from the climb, however, it would be that we all have within us the means to do, to accomplish, to become far more than we think. Climbing was the key for me; for others it will be different pursuits. But the important thing is that people acknowledge what they want to do, and then have the courage to go after it.

How often have you heard someone say, "What I'd really like to do is . . . ?" They say it, but they don't do it. What they'd really like may be to open a shop or a restaurant or to write or paint or make a movie or live in the wilderness or sail around the world or climb. It makes no difference what these things are. People have dreams; they should pursue them.

Perhaps the dreams will not be possible, after all. Perhaps the people do not have the talent or the stamina or the resources. But perhaps they *do*. In either case, it is a crucial self-discovery to make, and far superior to settling for unrealized notions and needling dissatisfactions. The great challenge, the real embrace of life, it seems to me, is to become what we can.

What about my own life? Well, I'm still on my leave of absence from Ideal Toy (and expect to be twenty years from now). Not that I was unhappy there—far from it. But climbing the World Trade Center opened a new world of options for me. It gave me an opportunity to work for myself, something I always wanted. Since then, I've done two climbs for ABC and may do more; it still hardly seems possible that I could be paid for what gives me so much joy anyway, but there it is. I've lectured, made some appearances, done a little modeling, one television ad for a product I like. I've served as New York Mobilization Chairman for the National Hemophilia Foundation. I've taken up scuba diving. I've made a down payment, with Jery, on a rolling piece of land in New York State, where we plan to build our own houses. I have the same friends, although I've made a few new ones. I still live in the same apartment in Queens. I certainly haven't gotten rich. Whenever I can get away, I still go climbing at the Gunks.

As a result of what came my way through the climb, my interests and aims have been changing. Working in film seems more appealing to me all the time. With that in mind—and with great enjoyment—I've been learning stunts, and studying acting. Where it will all lead I don't know. The uncertainty, the excitement of new possibilities, the risk are part of the adventure. My life to the end of the climb is one story. What has happened since is only the beginning of another.

The New

VOL. CXXVI....No. 43,588   © 1977 The New York Times Company   — NEW YORK, FR

Climber Conquers 110-Story Towe

ork Times

CITY EDITION

Weather: Mostly sunny today; mild tonight. Sunny, warmer tomorrow. Temperature range: today 57-77; yesterday 65-84. Details, page A23.

27, 1977 —

25 cents beyond 50-mile zone from New York City, except Long Island. Higher in air delivery cities.

20 CENTS

e 32,000 ground troops from Korea over

BY CHARLES MOHR

te on the bill was 326 to 49,

NEW YORK POST WALL ST. LATEST STOCKS

SUPER 'FLY' CLIMBS TRADE CENTER

HIGH DRAMA IN WORDS & PICTURES
PAGES 3, 9, 22, 28 & 29

HUMAN FLY!
To the Top of the World!

nding for 17 water projects that s to kill and $400 million he to eliminate in aid to "impacted" districts, or those with a high on of Federal employees. The impact aid funds were included in the H.E.W. bill approved by the committee

merican people. It is now up nate to protect the breathing

od Omen for Senate Seen

Special to The New York

WASHINGTON, May 26
Young flew back today from a trip to Africa and Britain, in the last 24 hours